First published in September 2013

A catalogue record for this book is available from the British Library

ISBN 978 0 85733 373 5

Library of Congress control no. 2013934887

Published by Haynes Publishing,
Sparkford, Yeovil,
Somerset BA22 7JJ, UK.
Tel: 01963 442030 Fax: 01963 440001
Int. tel: +44 1963 442030 Int. fax: +44 1963 440001
E-mail: sales@haynes.co.uk
Website: www.haynes.co.uk

Haynes North America Inc.
861 Lawrence Drive, Newbury Park,
California 91320, USA.

Printed in the USA by Odcombe Press LP,
1299 Bridgestone Parkway, La Vergne, TN 37086.

Acknowledgements

With thanks to:
Silverline Wheels and Tyres.
Ed Cobley.
Ian Corfield.
Land Rover Experience of England.

Unless otherwise stated, all photographs appearing in this manual are copyright of the authors, Vince Cobley and Dave Phillips.

driving and traction aids are often remarkably similar too.

Commuting to the office, taking an activity weekend away or collecting the kids from school are all things that four-wheel-drive vehicles do very well, but such tasks hardly test its all-terrain ability and are only the starting point as far as your 4x4's full capabilities are concerned. That vehicle parked outside your house is capable of taking you across continents, up mountains, through rivers and generally to the sort of places ordinary vehicles can't reach.

Whether or not you intend to make use of your 4x4's full potential, it's a good idea to understand how the vehicle works, understand the techniques involved to enable you to traverse various terrain and how the differing features and capabilities can be utilised.

This introduction is a generic guide to the basics. With so many vehicles, power, transmissions and many other options available it would be difficult, if not impossible, for us to go into lots of detail regarding every single option available. Besides, it's much more important that we provide you with an understanding of your vehicle's 4WD controls, driving techniques and the need for responsible driving to minimise environmental impact.

This book will act as a reference before and during future off-road adventures. So whatever the intended purpose for your chosen 4x4 vehicle, please read, learn, and go off and enjoy your vehicle more – go and *get muddy!*

RESPECT THE ENVIRONMENT

A four-wheel-drive vehicle can reach areas not accessible in conventional vehicles, putting the onus on the driver for responsible conservation of the environment in which such vehicles operate. Irresponsible off-road driving can potentially cause serious threats to the environment, such as:

- Physical erosion or damage to the ground, tracks, undergrowth and trees.
- Disturbances to and disruption of wildlife living and breeding habitats.
- Damage to sites of historical, archaeological or scientific significance.
- Pollution – noise, air and water.

It also seriously damages relationships with those people who seek to enjoy the environment in less intrusive ways.

Considerate and responsible off-road driving practice is actually little more than common sense. Primarily, it requires following some basic guidelines, such as:

- Know your rights of way and access and follow the Country Code. For example, if you're in doubt about access rights to a country track, check before you drive.
- Give priority to wildlife and livestock that you encounter.
- Respect the peace and tranquillity of others.
- Seek the best route to minimise erosion and damage to the landscape.
- Never, under any circumstances, leave litter or try burying or burning it – take it home with you.
- Drive with care, courtesy and consideration at all times.

Chapter One

Knowing your vehicle

OPPOSITE Understanding your vehicle's mechanics, some basic vehicle preparation and some driver training will ensure that in the future you will enjoy many miles of safe and rewarding off-road driving.

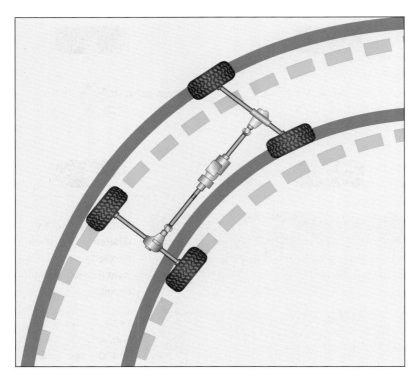

- To transmit the engine power to the wheels.
- To act as the final gear reduction in the vehicle, slowing the rotational speed of the transmission one final time before it hits the wheels.
- To transmit the power to the wheels while allowing them to rotate at different speeds – *ie* when cornering.

When a four-wheel vehicle turns, the outside wheels travel a longer distance than the inside ones. The differential in the axle will compensate for the extra distance that the outside wheel travels compared to the inside one. But in poor traction conditions, when one wheel starts to spin the differential will always send the power to the wheel with the least resistance.

On a 4x4 there are two types of four-wheel drive available – part-time and full-time.

Part-time 4WD is found on early Series Land Rovers, some Toyotas, Suzukis, Vauxhall Fronteras and Jeeps, to name a few. It allows a vehicle to be driven in the two-wheel-drive mode for everyday driving. The benefits of part-time 4WD are that it reduces drivetrain resistance and tyre wear for improved fuel economy and tyre life. However, four-wheel drive can be engaged when extra traction is needed: for example, when driving off-road, on surfaces with extreme articulations, on gravel, snow, ice or mud.

How your 4x4 works

It's a common misconception that '4x4' means that all four wheels are turning at the same speed simultaneously. They don't. If they did, the transmission would destroy itself very quickly. Let us explain...

All cars have a differential. The differential has three jobs:

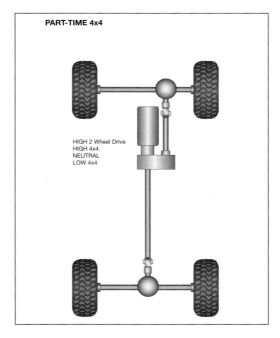

PART-TIME 4x4

HIGH 2 Wheel Drive
HIGH 4x4
NEUTRAL
LOW 4x4

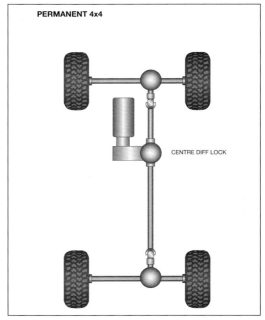

PERMANENT 4x4

CENTRE DIFF LOCK

Part-time 4WD vehicles are in high box most of the time, meaning the transmission sends all of the drive available to one axle (on most 4x4s it's the rear axle, although occasionally it's the front axle – check your vehicle's manual). When the conditions or terrain require it, full four-wheel drive must be engaged; here the transmission, via prop shafts and a transfer gearbox, splits the drive equally 50/50 to the front and rear axles.

Vehicles with part-time 4WD also have a second gearbox, known as a transfer gearbox, that splits drive torque transmitted between the front and rear axles.

On some vehicles the vehicle must be stationary or travelling slower than 2mph before the transfer case can be shifted from 2WD into 4WD. On others the transfer case can be shifted on the go, regardless of speed. It's important you know which category your vehicle falls into, so refer to its handbook.

Vehicles with part-time four-wheel drive may have manual or automatic locking hubs on the front wheels. These must be engaged at the same time as 4WD is selected to change from two-wheel to four-wheel drive. With manual locking hubs (often known as freewheeling hubs), you have to get out of the vehicle and twist a knob on both hubs, by hand or with a spanner, to engage the front wheels. To disengage freewheeling hubs you have to manually turn them to off or, when 2WD is selected, simply reverse for a short distance.

On 4x4s with full-time 4WD the front hubs don't disengage. Instead they turn the front driveshafts at all times. On most you can also select low-range or high-range gears. The low range are for precision and ultimate control when working and driving on rough off-road terrain.

The high range in part-time 4WD is engaged for driving at faster speeds on gravel tracks, snow-covered roads, or any surface offering poor traction.

However, without traction aids like auto-locking differentials in axles, or ABS-operated electronic traction control on modern vehicles, the best you can expect from most part-time 4WDs when in high or low gearbox is one-wheel drive at each axle. This is because the differential will always send the drive to the wheel with the least resistance.

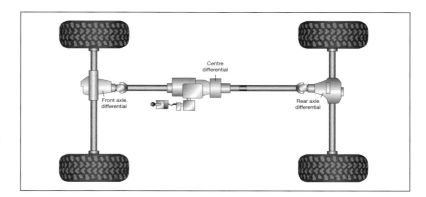

ABOVE The centre differential transfers torque to both front and rear axles simultaneously.

LEFT A freewheeling hub, showing 'Lock' and 'Off' positions.

Transmission wind-up

When a vehicle is travelling in a straight line all four wheels rotate at the same speed, but during cornering each wheel travels at a different speed due to the radius of the turn. The outside wheels have further to travel, and therefore must rotate faster than the inner wheels. Because of this, vehicles have a differential to allow the

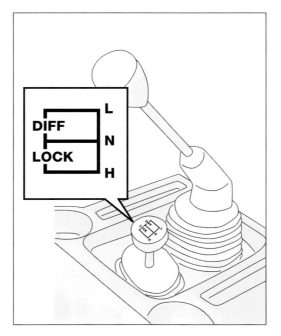

LEFT A Land Rover Defender and Discovery 'High', 'Low' and 'Diff Lock' engagement lever.

wheels on the same axle to rotate at different speeds. On 4x4s with full-time four-wheel drive, a centre differential is fitted to allow for different speeds between front and back wheels.

In a straight line, the centre diff transfers 50% drive to the front axle and 50% to the rear axle. But when the vehicle turns and is no longer travelling in a straight line the axles turn at different speeds. On a tight right turn, for instance, the front axle may require 65% of the drive and the rear axle 35%. But in part-time 4WD this doesn't happen – instead both axles still get sent 50% of the drive each. This creates the phenomenon known as axle wind-up or transmission wind-up, in which high strain is placed on the driveshaft and transmission, eventually causing one of two things to happen: either one of the wheels slips or spins to overcome the stress, or the driveshaft/transmission breaks. This is why caution should be taken when part-time 4WDs are driven on high-traction surfaces. On low-traction surfaces the transmission can unwind

itself by spinning wheels (a bit like a wound-up clock spring), thus reducing or eliminating any damage wind-up can cause.

How do you know you have wind-up? The steering becomes heavy, the steering wheel tries to straighten itself out, the gears are harder to locate, the friction in the transmission causes the vehicle to slow quicker than normal and you can hear – and sometimes see – your rear wheels slipping off the excess wind-up.

How do you get rid of transmission wind-up? If it's safe to do so, engage reverse and drive the vehicle backwards in a straight line until the transmission feels free.

So if your vehicle has permanent four-wheel drive (eg Land Rover Defenders, Mercedes 4x4s, some Jeeps and Toyotas), how come they don't get transmission wind-up if most of the time they're working on high-traction surfaces? The answer is that they have a central differential in the transmission to overcome this problem. This is necessary to compensate for the different speeds at which the front and rear wheels rotate when turning a tight corner.

However, a permanent 4WD can lose drive to all but one of its wheels, because the centre differential acts the same way as the differential in an axle does, but instead of sending the drive to the wheel with the least resistance it sends the drive to the axle with the least resistance and then on that axle to the wheel with the least resistance. This is why permanent 4WDs have a centre differential lock that locks the centre diff and makes it like a *part-time* four-wheel drive in 4WD mode, with again 50% of the drive going to the front axle and 50% going to the back axle. When the centre differential is locked, transmission wind-up can take place. On some vehicles, like the Land Rover Defender, it's easy to know when this happens because, when you disengage the centre differential lock, if the warning light in the instrument housing doesn't go out this means the torque twist and increased friction won't allow the gears to disengage. Reversing the vehicle until the light goes out will cure the problem.

But in reality, when a permanent 4WD has the centre diff locked it's the same as a part-time 4WD and the best you can expect without any traction aids is two-wheel drive – one front and one back wheel driving when traction is lost. One wheel on each axle spins while the

BELOW Transmission wind-up is caused by the front and rear axles requiring different percentages of drive, but receiving equal amounts. To avoid transmission wind-up on high-traction surfaces, try to drive in as straight a line as possible.

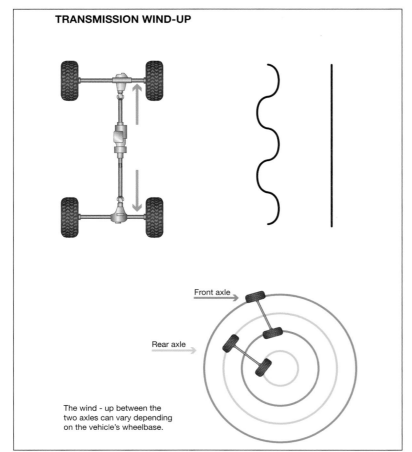

TRANSMISSION WIND-UP

Front axle

Rear axle

The wind - up between the two axles can vary depending on the vehicle's wheelbase.

other receives no drive at all due to the action of the axle differential. The exception to this is where a limited-slip or locking differential is fitted. A limited-slip diff allows a limited amount of drive to be applied to the stationary wheel before the other wheel on the same axle spins. A locking diff allows no slip at all and both wheels on the same axle turn at the same speed, regardless of the amount of traction.

Viscous coupling

A viscous coupling is often found integrated into the centre differential of some permanent 4WD vehicles. A viscous coupling is a mechanical device which transfers torque and rotation by using a viscous fluid. It consists of a number of circular plates with perforations, fitted very close to each other in a sealed drum. Alternate plates are connected to each output shaft leading to the front and back axles. The drum is filled with a fluid, often silicone-based, that thickens under stress.

When the two sets of plates are rotating in unison, the fluid stays cool and remains liquid. Under normal conditions both sets of plates and the viscous fluid spin at the same speed. But when one set of wheels tries to spin faster, perhaps because it's slipping, the set of plates corresponding to those wheels spins faster than the other set. The viscous fluid between the plates tries to catch up with the faster plates, dragging the slower plates along. This transfers more torque to the slower-moving wheels – ie the wheels that aren't slipping. The faster the plates are spinning relative to each other, the more torque the viscous coupling transfers. The coupling doesn't interfere with turns because the amount of torque transferred during a turn is so small. However, this also highlights a disadvantage of the viscous coupling: no torque transfer will occur until a wheel actually starts slipping.

A simple experiment with an egg will help explain the behavior of the viscous coupling. If you set an unboiled egg on the kitchen table, the shell and the yolk are both stationary. If you suddenly spin the egg, the shell will be moving at a faster speed than the yolk for a second, but the yolk will quickly catch up. To prove that the yolk is spinning, once you've got the egg spinning quickly stop it and then let go – the egg will start to spin again.

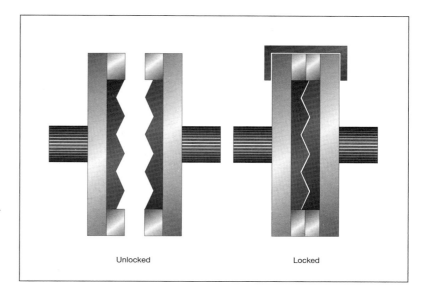

Unlocked   Locked

ABOVE The principle of how a locking differential operates.

Traction control

You'll see the term 'traction control' when you look at traction and handling aids in conjunction with a modern 4x4 vehicle. Traction control (called electronic traction control, or ETC, by some manufacturers) is one of those features that you don't think too much about until you need it; when you switch on your ignition you probably see the initials 'TC' illuminate on the dash, or you may have been close to getting stuck in soft ground with wheels slipping and seen 'TC' flashing.

So what exactly is traction control? Basically, traction control utilises the vehicle's anti-lock braking system (ABS) to detect and control wheelspin. Sensors constantly monitor the speed of each wheel. If one wheel is turning faster than its counterpart on the opposite side of the vehicle, the TC system pulses the brake on the faster-spinning wheel in an attempt to slow it down and transfer power to the wheel with better traction.

Traction control can be a big help when you're driving on snow or other slick surfaces, or when a wheel spins when accelerating from a standstill. But it's not without its flaws. In certain conditions, like sand, the TC can act like an anchor and slow the vehicle down when you're trying to maintain momentum to prevent your vehicle from getting stuck. That's why many experienced desert drivers disconnect traction control on their 4x4s – when faced with miles of dunes driving, for example.

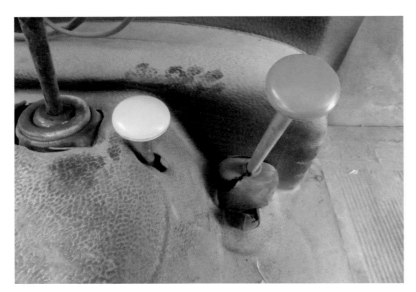

ABOVE Land Rover
Series I, II, IIA and III
'High', 'Low' and '4WD'
gear selection levers.

High- and low-range gearboxes

To enable a 4x4 to travel at lower speeds while
traversing rough terrain it needs lower gear
ratios. Not all 4WDs have low-range gearing
(the Land Rover Freelander, for example), and
this restricts their ability to tackle very rough
terrain. However, 4WDs that lack low-range
gearing are generally not built for severe off-
road conditions, or are sometimes fitted with a
'crawler' first gear to compensate for the lack
of low range. On most vehicles you have to be
stationary or travelling at very low speeds when
changing from high to low range, so we would
advise you to refer to the owner's manual for
your vehicle before attempting this.

The high-range ratios in 4WD mode are the
same as the gear ratios when in 2WD, but a
point worth mentioning is that you cannot select
low gearbox in 2WD mode in older Series Land
Rovers. When low-range 4WD is selected,
the gear ratios are approximately half those of
high range. You don't have to use low range
as soon as you put the vehicle in 4WD, but
only if the terrain requires it, although the exact
gear you require varies depending on vehicle
manufacturer and what power and torque your
engine has available.

For example, this means that a vehicle
travelling at 50mph in high-range fifth gear would
have an engine speed of 2,800 revs, but when
in low range at the same engine speed and the
same gear the speed would be around 24mph.

The many gearing options found in 4WD
vehicles help a vehicle tackle the unique
situations encountered while driving off-road.
The following are a variety of conditions in
which you'd want to use 4WD to avoid sliding
or spinning:

High-range 4WD
4H allows you to drive full speed, if necessary
and if the terrain allows. The high-range ratios
in 4WD mode are the same as the gear ratios
in 2WD.

When to use 4WD high
- For traction when the area is slippery but isn't steep.
- When stuck in sand.
- Extremely slippery conditions, like snow-covered roads.
- Ice.
- Shale and gravel tracks.
- Extremely muddy areas, to gain momentum.

The speed you travel must be dictated by the
severity of the terrain and the traction available.
High box will give you more traction over 2WD
and more momentum when required.

Low-range 4WD
4L is for driving at slow speed, giving you more
control and a better chance to read the ground
ahead. It reduces the strain on your vehicle.
But remember to stay below the recommended
maximum speed when in low range. While it
doesn't provide more traction, it does provide
two to three times more torque at half the
speed (or less) than high range. Low-range gear
ratios are usually about half those of high range.

When to use 4WD low
- On wet, slippery surfaces.
- Passing through sandy areas.
- Rough tracks.
- Shallow water.
- Rock-climbing.
- Through mud.
- Descending and climbing steep hills.

Additional tips
Don't change gears in the middle of a water
crossing, going up or down hills, on mud or in

sand dunes – in fact, as a general rule never change gear when the engine and transmission are under load.

- Be prepared: engage low-range 4WD before you need it.
- Don't operate part-time 4WD on hard, dry surfaces for a long period of time – you could cause transmission wind-up.
- When in doubt, look and risk-assess – and use a lower gear.

Terrain Response

It doesn't look much: it's just a simple knob that you turn to dial in the driving conditions you're facing. But since Terrain Response was introduced by Land Rover on the Discovery 3 model in the early years of the 21st century it's changed the face of off-road driving, and encouraged other manufacturers to develop and introduce similar systems.

It's impossible within the confines of this book to list every feature of every model. Here we'll just describe the original Terrain Response system, as installed in the Discovery 3 in 2004, because it's typical of the sort of system you'll now find on other models. As always, check your owner's handbook for the full spec for your vehicle.

The Terrain Response knob allows you to dial in the terrain you're about to drive, tailoring the engine management system of your vehicle to the optimum for those conditions. In developing this system, Land Rover's engineers analysed the characteristics of nearly 500 types of off-road surface, and determined the vehicle system inputs necessary to optimise performance on each.

For the driver, it helps you get the best out of the vehicle whatever the conditions, on- or off-road. It also removes most of the decision-making, which admittedly can be bewildering to newcomers to 4x4s. As a result it has certainly encouraged more people to take their 4x4s off-road. Off-roading used to have a sort of 'black arts' image that sounded too complicated and dangerous, but this new technology made it more accessible. These days off-road sites are full every weekend, with owners of new vehicles confidently giving it a try.

Some people thought it would take the skill

LEFT A Discovery 3 Terrain Response control.

out of off-road driving, but that hasn't been the case. No matter how advanced the technology, you still need a good driver to understand how to get the best out of it. The pre-selected settings aren't foolproof. The rest is up to you.

The downside is that it can potentially give novice drivers capabilities far greater than their own driving skills warrant. One of the biggest dangers these days is the inexperienced driver who speeds into the most difficult parts of an off-road course in the mistaken belief that Terrain Response will pull him through. It won't. Only good driving will do that.

The 'General' setting (special programs off) is what you should use on hard, non-slippery surfaces like farm tracks. It's suitable for all driving conditions where it isn't necessary to select a special program – ie surfaces that closely match a hard road surface; dry cobbles, tarmac, wooden planks, hard supportive surfaces with no loose coating of water, dust or similar material.

First you need to understand what it does. For example, in the 'Mud and Ruts' setting the computer system automatically switches on Hill Descent Control and changes the preload settings in the transmission and traction control to prevent excessive wheelspin. In most circumstances that's ideal, but in others it can create problems by reducing power just when you need it most.

Incidentally, the 'Mud and Ruts' setting isn't just for crossing ground which is muddy or deeply rutted. It's also for ground that's possibly

ABOVE Terrain
Response has a
setting for most
ground conditions.

ABOVE RIGHT
Discovery 3 'High–
Low' control lever,
with suspension
adjustment control.

soft and uneven to the point of maximum axle displacement. This unevenness could be brought about by sizeable wooden debris in the form of roots, brushwood and small logs. Despite its name, 'Mud and Ruts' isn't always the best setting for driving deep ruts. If your wheels aren't perfectly straight in the ruts, TR will think you're skidding and reduce power. Use 'General' setting and engage diff lock instead.

The 'Grass–Gravel–Snow' program can be selected when the underlying ground is firm, but there may be a coating of other material that can give a tendency to slip: water, slime, grass, snow, loose gravel, shale or pebbles, or even a thin coating of sand. This program should also be selected in icy conditions. In this mode the accelerator is mapped for more progression (helping to reduce wheelspin), the gearbox selects second gear high range or third gear low range, and traction control is more aggressive. In a manual gearbox vehicle the message board will advise setting off in third gear if low range is engaged.

In 'Rock Crawl' mode, or on unyielding ground – clusters of boulders, for example – which demands high levels of road-wheel displacement and careful vehicle control, the engine management system changes the accelerator pedal map for best slow-speed control. This means it's a great setting to employ in most precision driving situations, with the exception of trailer reversing, when you don't want diff lock engaged. For trailer reversing, just use the 'General' setting, in conjunction with low box.

'Rock Crawl' isn't available on the Freelander 2, because it doesn't have a low-ratio gearbox

for very slow driving, nor the extreme axle articulation and ground clearance of its larger stablemates. It's designed for slow, precision driving across a pile of boulders, but also invaluable for ditch and gully crossings.

The 'Sand' program is for soft and predominantly dry, yielding sandy ground, such as beaches, dunes and sand deserts, and can also be used in areas of deep gravel. The automatic transmission gives later up changes and earlier down changes to keep the engine running in its maximum power band. No HDC is engaged, and the initial throttle response is soft but becomes more aggressive as more pedal is applied. This setting can sometimes be used if you have a short run up to a steep or slippery hill, when the aggressive throttle response assists rapid acceleration and, with the gearbox staying in gear longer, can only help in this situation.

Hill Descent Control

Hill Descent Control (HDC) allows a smooth and controlled hill descent off-road in rough terrain without the driver needing to touch the brake pedal. It's another innovation introduced by Land Rover – in this case on the original Freelander, in 1997. (Other manufacturers' names for this include Hill Mode Descent Control and Downhill Assist.)

Before HDC, a manual form of control was used by some experienced drivers: called cadence braking, this involves the driver gently and constantly tapping the brake pedal to bring the vehicle to a contolled stop. HDC, on the other hand, is automatically engaged when

certain programs on the Terrain Response are engaged – a tell-tale illuminated symbol of a vehicle facing downhill will be seen on the dashboard. When it's on the vehicle will descend using the ABS braking system and wheel speed sensors to control each wheel's speed. If the vehicle accelerates without driver input, the system will automatically apply the brakes to slow down to the desired vehicle speed; if it senses a wheel locking up it automatically releases the brakes to avoid a skid. HDC normally has a set target speed of around 2–3mph, but should the ground conditions require a slightly higher or lower vehicle speed then the cruise control buttons can be used to adjust the speed to a desired level. Applying pressure to the accelerator or brake pedal will override the HDC system.

With Hill Descent Control, drivers can be confident that even a ride down hills with slippery or rough terrain will be smooth and controlled, and that they'll be able to maintain control as long as sufficient traction exists. But it's only as good as the traction available allows it to be; on low-traction surfaces – like downhill on ice – it will be of little use.

Dynamic Stability Control

Dynamic Stability Control (DSC) reduces engine power and applies ABS braking to individual wheels to help maintain control; it does this automatically via sensors and the traction control should it detect a loss of lateral grip that could occur in a turn. In Terrain Response the capability of the DSC in some settings is reduced. Never turn it off on the road but make

sure you turn it off for any off-road work requiring momentum – especially sand and mud. If not you'll find you go nowhere quickly, because with steering-wheel direction changes and wheels spinning the DSC is fooled into thinking the car is in a skid and applies the brakes to the spinning wheels. Just at the moment that you require momentum, the vehicle's computer applies the brakes, causing a loss of momentum and possibly getting you stuck.

Doing it the old-fashioned way

If your 4x4 doesn't have electronic management systems like traction control and Terrain Response you'll have to rely upon your own judgement. But that's not a great disadvantage. If your 4x4 has a low-range gearbox and centre-locking diff – like most Land Rovers, for example – you know you have the most important tools in the off-road driver's armoury.

On a steep downhill section you can use cadence braking, which means putting the vehicle in low box, selecting first or second gear and then, on the way down the hill (traction allowing), gently and continually dabbing the brake – just enough to hold the vehicle at a controllable speed.

Then there's manual traction control. If your wheels are spinning on some terrain it's possible to keep your right foot on the throttle to maintain enough engine revs to stop the engine stalling, then with your left foot gently brake, which fools a differential into sending the drive to the wheel with more grip. This works bests in automatics, but often works with manual boxes, too.

ABOVE Modern electronic handling systems like Land Rover's Dynamic Stability Control allow 4x4s with a high centre of gravity to corner without the excessive body roll experienced by older models.

Chapter Two

Suspension and articulation

OPPOSITE Your 4x4's ability to traverse uneven ground is enhanced by the articulation of its suspension system, although with modern traction aids, a high degree of articulation is not such a necessity..

Suspension is the term given to various springs, shock absorbers and linkages that connect the vehicle to its wheels and allows motion between the two. It has three main jobs: to smooth out bumps, keep tyres in contact with the road, and control vehicle stability. It also helps with stability under braking and protects loads and occupants, keeping them comfortable and reasonably well isolated from road noise, bumps and vibrations. We're not going to go into spring rates, rebounds and highly-technical suspension specs and data here, but it's worth remembering that having a good set of springs and shock absorbers is fundamental to safe and enjoyable on- and off-road driving.

Also bear in mind that there's a wealth of choice out there from specialist companies that offer high-performance alternatives to the suspension fitted to standard 4x4s. The manufacturer of your four-wheel drive will most likely have reached a compromise between the sort of suspension set-ups best for on- and off-road driving, but you may wish to replace it with springs and shock absorbers to enhance off-road ability. These include extreme systems for maximum wheel articulation on very uneven ground, for example. There's a wealth of choice available and our recommendation is to seek the expert advice of the specialist suppliers who'll be able to suggest a suitable set-up for your vehicle.

Suspension systems can be basically classified into two subgroups: dependent and independent. These terms refer to the ability of opposite wheels to move independently of each other.

Dependent suspension normally has a beam axle (likened to a cart axle) that holds wheels parallel to each other and perpendicular to the axle. When the camber of one wheel changes, the camber of the opposite wheel changes in the same way. Independent suspension, on the other hand, allows wheels to rise and fall on their own without affecting the opposite wheel.

Shock absorbers

Put simply, the shock absorbers damp out the up-and-down motions of a vehicle on its springs. They must also damp out much of the wheel bounce when the unsprung weight of a wheel bounces up and down on the springiness of its tyres. Some have suggested that the regular bumps found on dirt roads and in desert conditions (usually known as 'corrugations') are caused by this wheel bounce. This may be true, but we're confident that much of it is caused by weather and erosion.

Coil springs

Made from a round bar of steel that's twisted into a spiral shape, coil springs can be made with a constant or variable spring rate. The strength of a coil spring depends on the

LEFT This wheel is in contact with the ground, with the suspension at full compression, providing resistance to the differential, so (on vehicles without traction control) no drive will be transmitted to the wheel.

diameter and length of the round steel bar, the number of coils and the diameter of the finished coil, as well as the quality and carbon content of the steel. The one thing to remember when off-road driving is that the coil springs are normally seated at the top end by compression, which means that if your suspension is worn or has excessive travel the spring can pop out of its seat and possibly rub on the tyre; more importantly it will cause bad, perhaps even dangerous, handling on the road. To cure this you can put a clip, hose clip or similar around the seat and the coil to hold it in place.

Coil springs offer the best ride when set up properly and can also make off-road driving more comfortable because of their greater flexibility. Coil-spring suspensions use a coil spring at each corner of a vehicle, with link arms in place to act as pivots. Most 4x4 set-ups use two to four link arms, to connect and secure the axle to the chassis.

Leaf springs

A leaf spring takes the form of slender arc-shaped lengths of spring steel, clamped together. The centre of the arc provides location for the axle, while tie holes are provided at either end for attaching it to the vehicle body. For very heavy vehicles, a leaf spring can be made from

several leaves stacked on top of each other in several layers, often with progressively shorter leaves. Leaf springs can serve locating, and to some extent damping, as well as springing functions. The inter-leaf friction also provides a damping action – in fact for suppleness off-road competitors of old used to strip, clean and oil the various leaves.

Note we said 'of old'. That's because leaf springs are mainly found on older 4x4s, like Series Land Rovers. Manufacturers of modern 4WDs tend to opt for more sophisticated suspension systems. But that doesn't mean there's anything wrong with leaf springs –

BELOW This wheel is not in contact with the ground, with the suspension on full travel, providing no resistance to the differential, so drive will be transmitted to the wheel.

far from it. There are several experienced overlanders, for example, who wouldn't dream of setting off for an adventure through the African bush on newfangled coil springs! They prefer leafs because they can be mended by a village blacksmith in the middle of nowhere – and who are we to argue!

Sorry, we digress. Back to the leaf spring, which can either be attached directly to the chassis at both ends or attached directly at one end, usually the front, with the other end attached through a shackle to a short swinging arm. The shackle takes up the tendency of the leaf spring to elongate when compressed and thus makes for softer springiness.

Today, leaf springs are still used in heavy commercial vehicles such as vans and trucks, and even railway carriages, but a lot less in 4x4s and modern cars. For heavy vehicles, they have the advantage of spreading the load more widely over the vehicle's chassis, whereas coil springs transfer it to a single point. Unlike coil springs, leaf springs also locate the rear axle, eliminating the need for trailing arms and a Panhard rod, thereby saving cost and weight in a simple live axle rear suspension.

A more modern implementation is the parabolic leaf spring. This design is characterised by fewer leaves, whose thickness varies from centre to ends, following a parabolic curve (hence the name). In this design, inter-leaf friction is unwanted, and therefore there's only contact between the springs at the ends and at the centre where the axle is connected. The end result is an improved performance compared to ordinary leaf springs, whose performance is often compromised by rusting between the individual leafs preventing proper movement. The ride from a vehicle on parabolic springs is often likened to that of coil springs.

Suspension travel

Suspension travel is the furthest distance suspension can travel and/or extend (like when the vehicle is on a jack and the wheel hangs freely or just off of the ground), and the suspension's compression is when the vehicle's wheel can no longer travel in an upward direction toward the vehicle or the shock absorber can no longer be compressed.

Bottoming or lifting a wheel could cause serious handling problems, or directly cause damage by allowing wheels to spin – then when the wheel comes into contact with the ground again and grips suddenly, this can put a strain on the half-shafts and diffs.

A lot of earlier off-road vehicles use what are known as 'limiting straps' to restrict the suspension's downward travel within safe limits for the linkages and shock absorbers; in some situations the shock absorber rod itself becomes the suspension's limit of travel, which it isn't designed to do and this can cause a breakage. These straps are still needed on some racing 4x4s, which are intended to travel over very rough terrain at high speeds. Without something to limit the travel the shock absorbers and suspension bushes would take all the force when the suspension reaches full

BELOW Vehicles with beam axles and coil-over-shock absorber suspension usually have a high degree of wheel travel.

BELOW RIGHT Vehicles with independent torsion-bar-type suspension usually have little wheel travel.

ABOVE Sometimes, a
suspension with a high
degree of articulation
is simply not enough...

droop, and it can even cause the coil springs
to come out of their seats if they're held in by
compression forces only. Excessive strain can
also be placed on propshaft universal joints,
causing excessive wear and tear.

The opposite of the limiting straps are
'bump-stops', which protect the suspension
and vehicle (as well as the occupants) from
violent bottoming, caused when the terrain
causes the suspension to run out of upward
travel without fully absorbing the energy of the
stroke in the shock absorbers. Without bump-
stops a vehicle that bottoms out will experience
a very hard shock when the suspension
contacts the bottom of the frame or body,
which is transferred to the occupants (mainly
through the back and the teeth!) and every
weld on the vehicle. Most 4x4 vehicles therefore
come with plain rubber pads to absorb the
worst of the forces and insulate the shock.

Roll weight or body roll is something the off-
road driver always needs to bear in mind. When
a vehicle corners its weight is transferred and
its springs compressed. Now, a compressed
spring will at some time need to rebound or
'un-compress', and the speed and rate it does
this will affect on- and off-road handling by
giving less downforce to one side of the vehicle,
and again giving the differentials a chance to
send drive to the wheels with less resistance.

Before all the electronic wizardry and
various traction aids were introduced, the
capability of a 4x4 vehicle was judged by its
ability to keep its wheels in contact with the
ground. Why? As we mentioned earlier, the
differential will always send the drive to the
wheel on an axle with the least resistance – so
the better your vehicle is at keeping its wheels
in contact with the ground, the better your
chances are of maintaining traction.

Chapter Three

Vehicle preparation

OPPOSITE Charles Morgan modified this Defender to transform it into an expedition-prepared vehicle in order to work alongside Vince leading convoys of 4x4 owners into the Moroccan Sahara.

All 4x4s should always be properly serviced and maintained, but for off-roading this is particularly important. This is how to prepare your off-roader for every eventuality…

Part 1: Vehicle maintenance

We always say that a well-maintained vehicle is much better than spending all your money on the fancy bits and bobs that many 4x4 owners can't resist. In the UK there's an astonishing amount of stuff you can accessorise your four-wheel drive vehicle with, particularly when it comes to models like the Land Rover Defender, which, thanks to its bolt-together simplicity, many people liken to a full-size Meccano set. In fact both the authors admit there have been occasions when we've perhaps been over-enthusiastic with the accessories...

But that's harmless fun, of course. The serious point we're making here is that some owners make their vehicles look the part (in their eyes) but cut corners when it comes to ensuring they have a well-serviced and prepared vehicle. There are no prizes for guessing which is the best option in the long run, both on- and off-road.

Generally, most 4WDs are tough vehicles that'll take a lot of abuse, but like all cars they must be properly serviced and maintained or they'll fail at the most inopportune moments, which can be at best inconvenient … at worst life-threatening. Think about it.

The 4x4 vehicle has more areas requiring oil to lubricate its many moving parts than a normal car, so ensure regular oil changes are made at the manufacturer's recommended intervals and that all levels are checked regularly. This is more so off-road especially, when the vehicle could be operating at low speeds and high revs, as well as at extreme angles, which of course all affect oil levels. For example, if you're climbing a steep hill it stands to reason that the oil level at the front of the sump, diff or whatever will be lower than at the back. The reverse would be true on a steep downhill slope.

It's the same with fuel. Back in the days when modified V8 Range Rovers were popular as off-road triallers, one of the pitfalls of severe hill climbs was that if your tank was low you only had the fuel in the bowl of your carburettor to get you to the top, as the steep angle of the vehicle left the pick-up point inside the tank high and dry! To avoid similar embarrassments, always make sure you have enough fuel in the tank when off-roading, as steep drops, climbs and side slopes can shift the fuel level away from pick-up points and in-tank fuel pumps.

Before going on any long journey, owners who drive off-road regularly in their 4x4s should ensure that the radiator and intercooler (where fitted) are clean and free of mud. It may not have any discernible effect when you're making short journeys locally, but on a long stint of motorway driving it could cause your vehicle to overheat and get damaged.

The best way of cleaning a radiator is with an ordinary hosepipe. Take your time to loosen and then wash away the softened mud. Don't attack it too close with a power-wash if that's all you have available, because the powerful force could damage the radiator fins.

If you've been driving in mud, clay or heavy sand – which is, in fact, most off-road conditions – you could find that the abrasive content of the soil particles has accelerated the wear of certain vehicle components with which it's come into contact, especially the brakes, some seals/gaiters around the axle, and the wheel hubs, which are obviously in close contact with mud etc. Hose them down gently and inspect them regularly, paying particular attention to brakes and bearings.

Bearing failure on the stub axle is common

BELOW Maintenance is a must. Wheel bearings should be checked on any vehicle that is used off-road regularly.

among those who do a lot of off-roading in muddy quarries. They're also subjected to water and dirt ingress. Check them by jacking up the vehicle securely, holding the wheel top and bottom and checking for play. If it's excessive, change the bearings.

Many 4x4s, including Land Rover Defenders, have taper bearings, which can be adjusted, but if there's any play at all it's worth stripping the hub down and changing them anyway. While you're there, ensure the seals are in good order too. The main thing to check is the reason for that play. Apart from natural wear and tear, a frequent major problem when off-roading is for the seal mating the axle to the brake disc casing to leak, allowing water and mud into the seal and on to the bearing, resulting in a very rapid wear rate.

When in doubt, always change the bearings. It's worth it for your peace of mind. If you've ever had a faulty wheel-bearing break up when you're travelling at speed, you'll know what we mean…

It's much the same story with propshaft universal joints. Check for signs of wear, excessive play and – a real giveaway, this – dryness. If it's dry, don't attempt to re-grease it – just change it, because the damage is almost certainly already done. An increase in transmission backlash can be a telltale sign that some transmission components, like universal joints, are wearing or worn.

Now check the differential oil seals and fluids. Obvious signs of problem areas are leaks around the diffs and the ends of the axle tubes; you can also look underneath the vehicle, and even up the back of the vehicle for oil slicks caused by the air turbulence spreading the oil as a spray underneath and up the rear of the vehicle as it travels along at a moderate speed.

If the seals are leaking, water can be drawn in. You'll soon know if there's been any water ingress by taking out the diff filler plug and checking the colour of the oil. If it's white and emulsified it means it's been contaminated by water – and requires changing immediately.

Also check for play in the drive flanges, suspension and shock absorbers. Unless the springs and shocks are relatively new, we'd change them anyway – for a long overland trip, for example. Standard suspension set-ups

are perfectly fine while they're working, but for long expeditions where the weight the vehicle carries is increased, or for more advanced off-road driving, we'd seek a specialist company and ask their advice about fitting bespoke springs and shock absorbers, designed for your requirements.

Turning to the cooling system, check all drive belts and hoses for cracks and signs of wear. If necessary, change the water pump and renew the gasket for overland trips. You want your cooling system in top condition if you're making overland journeys, especially in hot climates, to avoid overheating.

Off-roading puts extra wear on certain components, not least your alternator. Again, the ingress of dirt, dust and water can lead to premature failure, so if in doubt either fit a new one, or at least bring along a new one as a spare. An off-road play day can start the deterioration of the alternator with all the extra mud and water it takes in, so maintain it by gently hosing it down and applying WD40 or similar water dispersant.

Different engines have various drive belts for water pumps, power steering pump, alternators, etc. The engine bay is a dusty, dirty environment, especially when you're driving off-road. Belts do get brittle and wear over time, but this time period is considerably shortened when they get immersed in water, mud and dust, so once again check regularly for signs of wear and tear. It's well worth carrying spares on a long trip.

Air filters will suffer if you're travelling on dusty, dirty tracks. Before you leave on a long trip abroad, change the existing one and bring along at least one spare. In dusty conditions, check it daily. Also check it after fording streams and rivers: if the filter gets soaked, it'll restrict airflow to the engine and reduce performance. If your driving does comprise a lot of driving in dusty conditions, or wading through water, it's well worth fitting a raised air intake. But more on this later.

On to the windscreen wipers. Have you renewed them in the last six months? If not, do so now, with top-quality replacements. Don't skimp on this. Wherever you take you 4x4 – round the world or down the road to the local supermarket – you should have perfect vision through the windscreen at all times. It amazes us to see the number of drivers who don't bother to change their wiper blades until they're falling apart and leaving horrible smears across the screen. They're among the cheapest and easiest of items to change on any vehicle.

If it's wet and rainy during your travels – and in some countries, at certain times of the year, you'll experience monsoon conditions and mud – you may want to change the wiper blades even more often. New ones are usually easy to obtain in most parts of the world, just as they are in service stations in the UK, but bring along spares just in case. They're light and don't take up much room in your vehicle. And don't forget the rear wipers (where fitted).

Talking of overland travel, are your brake pads thick enough to last the duration of the trip? If not, change them. And bring spares anyway. Driving twisting mountain passes will greatly increase brake wear … and a heavily-laden expedition vehicle will result in even more. Remember that in many Third World countries even the major roads are in effect off-road tracks, by European standards.

Give your exhaust system the once-over, paying attention to the brackets, mounting rubbers and general condition. If it fails abroad, it could prove very expensive to put right. If you plan to keep your vehicle for a few years, a stainless steel system may prove a sound investment.

You may think that a heavy towbar will add unwanted extra weight and plan to remove it for off-roading or long road trips, but our advice would be to keep it on. Not only does it offer a secure recovery point if you get stuck in a tricky off-road situation, it'll also offer some protection to the back of your vehicle in the event of an accident – an important consideration in those parts of the world where driving standards range from questionable to terrifying.

Part 2: Vehicle modifications

Suspension

Before venturing off-road, think about your suspension. While most modern 4x4 models should be capable without changes, older vehicles you intend to load up with extra weight will probably require renewed or upgraded suspension.

Remember that cheap is never best: a budget component that fails in the back of beyond isn't much of a bargain, is it? It could be hard to replace, too. Always buy reputable makes and the best you can afford.

Don't just guess at which uprated springs and shock absorbers to use, as the handling and performance of your vehicle depends upon you getting it dead right. Go to one of the specialists – they'll know exactly what combination of shock absorbers and springs will suit your vehicle and personal requirements. Even though we drive off-road virtually every day of the year and like to think we know a bit about 4x4s, we still turn to the experts when it comes to advice on setting up the suspension and handling of our vehicles.

Talking of suspension, there's then the question of how far to raise it. Raised suspension can be useful for off-roading or overland travel, to give you a little more ground clearance and help cope with heavy loads, but we'd advise no more than an inch or two or you risk upsetting the centre of gravity and making your vehicle unstable. This is especially so if you're travelling with roof tents and heavy loads like jerry cans on the roof – all of which have a drastic effect upon your 4x4's centre of gravity.

Remember that if you do fit suspension with a lift, or any specialised non-standard systems come to that, you may have real problems replacing broken components once you're abroad. You may have to bring along spares, just in case.

At home in the UK, you may use your 4x4 primarily as an off-roader and even use it to compete in off-road conditions. If performance in the rough is more important to you than impeccable road manners, you may opt to fit extreme suspension packages, which allow

you to keep your wheels in contact with the ground in the most demanding situations. But again, it should be fitted by a specialist – and remember that it'll definitely have an adverse effect upon on-road handling once you leave the off-road course. Many off-road competitors trailer their special vehicles to off-road sites for this reason.

Raised air intakes

A raised air intake – also known as a snorkel – isn't an off-road necessity, but it's very useful if driving in dusty conditions or fording rivers and streams. This means it's well worth fitting one for overland adventures, as well as general off-road driving.

Make sure you pick the right model for your vehicle and engine. You don't want to decrease airflow to the engine, as it'll reduce performance. Likewise, you can't risk water getting through the seals, as any water that gets into the engine will cause severe damage. If in doubt about your DIY abilities, get it professionally fitted.

Winches

A winch is very useful if you plan to drive off-road alone. Modern electric winches are reliable and easy to operate (as long as you follow all safety rules). Before fitting one, though, make sure the chassis is sound and able to take the immense forces generated. We once watched the owner of an elderly and unkempt Series III Land Rover get stuck in mud and attempt to winch it out, only to see the winch pull the front off his rusty chassis! A winch bumper should be well made and properly mounted to the chassis, which must be sound.

We recommend using an electric winch with a minimum of 8,000lb pulling capacity, loaded with around 25–30m of cable – either steel or synthetic. And make sure you also carry the proper winching kit, which includes heavy-duty gloves. We can't stress the safety aspect too highly: even among experienced off-roaders, accidents happen – and accidents involving winches can be very nasty indeed. They're immensely powerful bits of machinery. We once witnessed the horrific sight of an off-roader getting his thumb ripped off when his hand strayed too close to the winch he was operating. Incidents like that make us take winch safety issues very seriously indeed.

Remember that an electric winch imposes severe drain on your battery, so you may wish to fit a second, auxiliary battery to your vehicle to power the winch and lights etc, with a split-

ABOVE Raised air intakes allow a greater wading depth, and can help to draw in clean air in dusty conditions.

ABOVE LEFT Raised air intake joints must be sealed to prevent water ingress.

BELOW A winch can offer a controlled form of recovery in difficult situations.

ABOVE Heavy-duty spare-wheel carriers and rear racks can be useful, and roof tents can be mounted on suitable roof racks.

charging system. This means the cranking power of your main battery isn't adversely affected by winch operation.

Even if you don't fit a vehicle winch, you can carry a hand-operated Tirfor winch. But these are almost as expensive as the cheaper electric winches – and nearly as heavy – as well as taking up valuable space in the vehicle.

Roof racks

A good roof rack should be designed so that it spreads the load along the vehicle's guttering and has mounting points along the side. Avoid ones

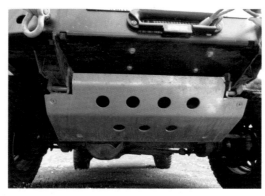

RIGHT Steering guards protect vulnerable steering components.

BELOW 'Rock sliders' protect sills and door bottoms.

that bolt together like Meccano sets, as they're prone to shake apart once you do any amount of driving over uneven surfaces ... which is exactly what you'll be doing off-road, of course.

The very best roof racks are usually made of aluminium or aluminium alloy, which are relatively light compared to their strength. There are some very good models available and some are specially designed to accommodate roof tents, which you'll probably consider if you're travelling through remote countries, or perhaps just for the fun of the great outdoors during a greenlaning jaunt.

Any equipment mounted on a roof rack must be properly secured with ratchet straps. As we've already mentioned, don't be tempted to put too much heavy equipment up there, as it'll make your vehicle top-heavy and upset the centre of gravity – which is particularly dangerous on severe side slopes. Check your vehicle manufacturer's advice for maximum loads on roof racks or rails.

Load security

This should always be high on your list of priorities, for safety reasons. Ensure that everything carried in the back of your 4x4 is stowed away in boxes, which in turn are secured by ratchet straps. You don't want heavy boxes sliding around in the back of your vehicle, because the shift in weight can be enough to tip it over, on a side slope for example.

Also, it's a good idea to fit a strong dog guard between the load area and passenger area, to keep people and heavy flying objects apart in the case of an accident.

Underbody protection

If you go off-road regularly, you may wish to protect your vehicle with what amounts to armour for the underside. First priority should be the exposed steering arms, which can be protected with a bolt-on protector, usually fabricated from alloy. Diffs and the fuel tank can be protected in the same way, and some off-roaders like to fit rock or tree sliders, which protect the sills.

Bolt-on protectors like these are produced by several aftermarket companies for vehicles commonly used off-road, like Land Rovers and Jeeps, but you may find it more difficult to buy

such items off the shelf for 4x4s that aren't such a common sight on the off-road course. For some models, you may even have to have them custom-made.

Lights

Driving lights on some older 4WDs can be quite puny by modern standards, so consider fitting extras. For off-road purposes it's useful to have them mounted on the roof, so that they're away from the mud and will stay cleaner, and therefore brighter, longer. This will also protect them from flying stones, etc. But in most European countries it's illegal to use roof-mounted lights on public highways, so don't be tempted to switch them on when you're back on tarmac (technically this includes green lanes with vehicular rights of way, as these are classed as public roads).

Part 3: Essential kit

There are some things in life you simply can't afford to be without. For the off-roading 4x4 owner, that means everything from clothing to winching kits. Let's go through them...

Clothing

We all know that 4x4s were designed to take us absolutely anywhere and everywhere. That means climates from a teeth-chattering -40°C to a baking 40°C plus, including wet greenlaning weekends in Wales, winters in deep mud at the off-road site, sticky jungle drives, and hot, arid travel in the desert. That means you won't find any clothing to suit all the conditions you're likely to encounter in your adventures, but there are some principles you can follow wherever you go.

First, adopt the layers principle – that means lots of thin, breathable layers of clothing made of modern fabrics. They'll keep you warmer in cold climates and, strangely enough, cooler in hot ones. This is mainly because they act like a wick, taking moisture away from your body. It's that moisture – mainly your own perspiration – that makes you feel either clammy and sweaty in hot climates or cold and shivering in cold ones.

Outdoor shops and Internet suppliers that specialise in catering for hikers and climbers are the places to look for this clothing, which isn't necessarily expensive. While you're there, make sure you get a good, waterproof outer layer. Modern fabrics like Gore-Tex are ideal and in our opinion much better than the old waxed cotton we used to wear to keep the rain out.

The same applies to boots. It's a matter of personal taste and comfort, but hiking-style boots or wellies will keep the wet out. Trainers may be comfortable for driving in, but once you're out of the vehicle in the typically muddy terrain of an off-road site they may not be such a good choice.

Ex-Army clothing is cheap and hard-wearing, and traditionally popular with UK off-roaders, but not nearly as good as proper outdoor clothing made from modern synthetic fabrics. That, after all, is why some British soldiers prefer to buy their own kit rather than rely upon the inadequate stuff supplied by the stingy government...

Ex-military clothing is also a definite no-no in many countries around the world. In fact, in some it's banned. With military coups not exactly rare in some African countries, you can see why they're wary of men in 4x4s wearing camo clothing. Nobody with any sense of regard for their own safety would drive through the

ABOVE LEFT Fitting a differential protector.

ABOVE Additional roof-mounted lights can be useful in many situations.

developing world in this sort of stuff. Incidentally, the same applies to the vehicles themselves: for example, in many countries driving an ex-military Land Rover or Jeep with a camo paint job is likely to attract the wrong sort of attention from the authorities and locals. Our advice: just don't.

As an aside, it's a similar story even in the UK. Drive down a country byway in a normal Land Rover wearing normal clothing and the odds are that a passing farmer will smile and wave. Try the same thing in a modified off-roader with camo clothing and you'll get a very different reception, because in the farmer's eyes you just look like the sort of person who's going to behave irresponsibly. Don't ask us why, but it's a fact. Maybe we all judge people too much on appearances.

Personal stuff

First and foremost, get a good pair of sunglasses to wear while driving. Many opticians offer a pair of prescription sunglasses at a reduced price if you buy them at the same time as your normal specs. If you wear glasses, take advantage of such offers, because wearing high-quality shades suited to your own eyes will make driving safer and a lot less strain. Polarised lenses will cut down on glare.

Talking of sun, make sure you bring sun cream and/or sun block. The sun can be deceptive, particularly as you get near the equator. Back in 2000, Dave was driving an open-top Series I Land Rover through the mountains of Lesotho in Southern Africa. The sun was bright but the temperatures were only just above freezing, so he didn't bother to wear sun block. Big mistake! Within a couple of hours he was badly sunburnt – and to make matters worse hadn't even noticed until his travelling companions told him he had turned bright red! Even in the UK in winter you can get sunburn, especially if you're out in the open in mountainous country. Windburn is every bit as painful, so too is chapped skin from being out in the cold and rain, so make sure you've got hand cream, moisturiser and lip salve. If your macho mates laugh, let them. You'll be the one who's laughing when they ask to borrow it.

Food and drink

A well-equipped overland expedition will see your 4x4 become, literally, your home from home, with most likely a built-in gas cooker, sink, fridge, water tank and all manner of cupboards for storing cutlery, crockery, food and drink. A properly prepared Land Rover long-wheelbase Defender modified to conquer continents is a delight to see – but not on the off-road course, unless you like broken crockery and scrambled eggs. For the off-roader, a small gas stove and essential supplies in properly secured containers are the order of the day (unless there's a cafe on site, or course...).

On a greenlaning trip it's nice to be able to stop in a pleasant spot with a great view and brew up a cuppa on a gas or petrol-powered stove, or even a Kelly kettle, where by burning twigs and scraps of paper in the central 'chimney' you can boil up the water in the outer cylinder in no time. Whether you're crossing a continent or the Cotswolds, our advice is the same: bring along what you need, but stow it away carefully so it's not rattling around the vehicle. Everything should always be packed away and secured properly.

Bottled water is readily available in most countries, but check that the seals are intact. Back in 1998, shortly before we travelled to Malaysia for an off-road adventure in the tropical rainforests to the north of the country, Dave made an appointment at his local GP for the appropriate jabs and anti-malaria tablets. While there, his doctor told him to avoid water during the trip, and instead drink canned or bottled beer (in moderation). 'They can tamper with bottled water and refill the bottles with contaminated water, but they can't do that with beer,' he said. It was medical advice that Dave cheerfully followed during the trip (although Vince insists it was not always in moderation). In the absence of welcome, if unconventional, medical advice, you should perhaps take the more sober route of buying sterilising kits that allow you to treat water to make it safe to drink.

Emergency items

If you're on an expedition you're probably going to explore remote places far from medical facilities (which in some developing countries may be very basic anyway). We'd recommend anybody planning such a trip to enrol on a basic first aid course before they set off, and to read all the information you can glean from the Internet and specialist books. Type in 'overland medicine' on Google and you'll enjoy plenty of options.

Incidentally, you don't have to be in the middle of the jungle to be a long way from medical assistance. In the Welsh mountains and the Lake District, tracks can be remote – and mobile signals notoriously weak or non-existent – so a basic understanding of first aid is always a good idea. Even if you're going to the local off-road quarry, a basic first aid kit in your 4x4 is essential. Make sure it includes a selection of plasters, bandages and gauzes, antiseptic and eyewash. A fire extinguisher should always be carried if you're attempting extreme off-road challenges.

Blankets are also a must, and not just for cold climates and off-road driving in the winter months. Also make sure there are sleeping bags for all occupants. Even if you don't intend to camp out, you might get stranded somewhere remote and be forced to sleep in your vehicle.

Recovery equipment

Do you need a winch? It depends on what sort of terrain you'll be driving. If you're travelling alone we'd definitely recommend one, but make sure you're properly trained on how to use it safely before you set off. As we mentioned earlier, a winch is immensely powerful and can be very dangerous in the wrong hands. You'll also need a variety of strops, shackles, gloves and a choker chain, which is used on sharp rocks that would damage an ordinary strop. There won't always be a convenient tree or rock nearby if you do get stuck, so you may wish to bring along some kind of ground anchor … but remember that they're very heavy, and this sort of equipment will take up valuable space in your vehicle.

Whether or not you're driving a winch-equipped vehicle, you'll definitely need a basic recovery kit when you go off-roading. This includes a strong recovery rope, at least one shovel, a sledgehammer, a small axe, a saw and a machete.

Tools

Basic tools should include a good-quality socket set, a selection of spanners and screwdrivers. Many 4x4 owners prefer to carry a high-lift jack, but although these are very

LEFT Shackles must be suitably load-rated for their intended use.

versatile – they can be used like a winch to get you out of trouble if you're stuck in deep ruts, for example – they're also heavy and bulky and can be dangerous in the wrong hands. A heavy-duty bottle jack may be a safer option, and will certainly be lighter and take up less room.

Also useful are get-me-home repair kits, which include Radweld, metal bond, pipe and exhaust repair items and, of course, ever-versatile gaffer tape. Torches are essential. Bring along at least two, plus spare batteries. Vince also carries a wind-up torch, just in case.

ABOVE A minimum requirement for emergency items – recovery rope, fire extinguisher, shovel, shackles and first-aid kit.

LEFT Fitting a wading blanket to prevent water ingress into the engine compartment.

Chapter Four

Tyres

OPPOSITE Comparison between tyre capable of handling all terrain types (left) and one biased towards on-road performance (right).

Tyre choice is of great importance to the off-road driver. After all, it's the tyre that's your contact between your vehicle and the ground surface you're driving. To many over-enthusiastic 4x4 owners, that often means fitting the biggest, knobbliest tyres they can find – but that isn't usually the best answer, as we'll explain.

In fact, on modern 4x4s standard tyres are all you need in most off-road situations, thanks to new technology like the Terrain Response system fitted on most modern Land Rovers, which optimises all the vehicle's systems, including raising the suspension where necessary, to give a standard vehicle on road-pattern tyres the capability of accessing terrain that would have required a more aggressive tyre in the past. Other manufacturers have developed similar systems.

But, of course, not everybody drives new 4x4 models with that handy terrain dial. And there are certain situations where using specialist tyres will help you off-road regardless of what vehicle you're driving. There's a bewildering choice of rubber available for the off-roader, but we'll attempt to help you choose the right tyres for

your 4x4 that will enhance its off-road capability.

For example, in deep mud a mud tyre will always help you and prevent you from getting stuck. The chunky tread pattern means that it's 'self-clearing' (ie the tread won't get clogged up with mud), but one downside is that if not driven with care this type of tyre can cause damage to the surface you're driving on. The other downside is that they aren't so comfortable on tarmac surfaces, because there's less rubber in contact with the road. This can drastically affect braking distances on wet roads, and they tend to be noisy, so bear this in mind when considering buying ultra-knobbly rubber.

All-terrain tyres do exactly what their name suggests. They have a tread pattern somewhere between a road-biased tyre and a true mud pattern. They offer better grip than standard tyres in muddy conditions but are less aggressive and are less likely to damage the environment. They also have much better road-holding manners and are quieter than mud tyres.

Tyre design has come on in leaps and bounds in recent years, with the result that the

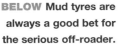

BELOW Mud tyres are always a good bet for the serious off-roader.

FAR LEFT The tread pattern on mud tyres helps to clear the tread in most conditions.

LEFT A standard-fitment tyre offers little tread clearing.

leading all-terrain tyres are now very capable in off-road situations. Couple this with excellent tarmac performance comparable to many road tyres, and they're a great choice. We won't mention specific brands here, but there's no doubt that the premium brands will last longer and perform better than the cheaper tyres from suppliers you've never heard of.

There's also the very important matter of safety: your tyres are your vehicle's only point of contact with the surface you're driving on. We don't want to sound over-dramatic, but your life depends on those bits of rubber. We reckon that's reason enough to stick with reputable brands, even if it does mean paying a little more. With tyres, like most other things in life, you get what you pay for.

To get better traction in some off-road situations, you can reduce the pressure in your tyres to give a greater 'footprint' – *ie* the area of tyre that's in contact with the ground. This

works well in soft sand and mud. You can reduce your tyre pressures to around 15psi, but ensure you have the means to pump them back to their normal pressures before you return to tarmac. If you're using a battery-operated compressor to re-inflate your tyres, make sure you buy a powerful one, as Land Rover tyres are invariably big and take a long time to pump up. We've seen quite a few of the cheaper 12V compressors literally burn out under the stress of trying to inflate big tyres.

Tyre types and construction

The modern tyre is a mixture of steel belts, advanced fabrics and each manufacturer's own top-secret compounds, which are made of around 40% natural rubber and 60% synthetic materials. Most manufacturers now include, among many others, a chemical called silica

BELOW This diagram shows the difference in construction between a radial tyre and a crossply tyre.

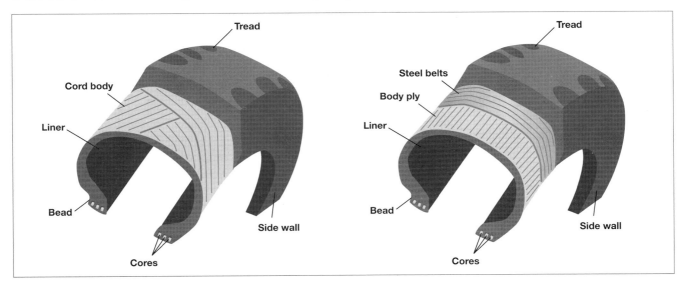

which, along with advanced tread design, helps to optimise the performance of the tyre in wet weather conditions.

Most modern cars, including 4x4s, run on radial tyres. Radial tyres wear much better than cross-ply tyres; they have better heat resistance and will improve your fuel economy. They also have a far greater structural rigidity for those times when cars are cornering and their tyres are deforming.

To check if you have radial or cross-ply tyres on your vehicle just look at the tyre-size marking on the tyre sidewall. For example, on a 195/50R15 tyre the letter 'R' indicates that this it's a radial type. But if the writing on the tyre states, say, 180/14-16, the hyphen symbol indicates that it's a cross-ply type.

A cross-ply tyre is made using a criss-cross pattern of cords that go diagonally at a 30°–40° angle. The tread is then applied to this pattern, forming the tyre. These tyres offer a smooth ride over rough and bumpy surfaces as this design lets the whole tyre flex easily. Because of the construction, sidewalls are normally stronger too, although a downside to this tyre technology, especially in today's environmentally-aware society, is increased rolling resistance, which means poorer fuel economy. Another downside is the loss of control and traction at faster speeds. That's why cross-ply tyres normally have a lower speed rating.

Radial tyres offer the best of both worlds. These tyres can be stronger in design and are fitted to most cars and other vehicles, as well as 4x4s. Radial tyres are made by the cords around the tyre going in the direction of travel. This reduces wear on the tyre, and the radial cords are in the sidewall, therefore allowing the tyre to spring and support the vehicle's weight. A radial tyre uses ply cords extending from the beads across the tread. The cords are laid from the centre of the tyre at right angles and parallel to each other as well as the stabiliser belts.

It's illegal both to fit cross-ply and radial tyres on the same axle and to fit cross-ply tyres on the rear axle with radials on the front axle.

Rolling resistance

Rolling resistance is the resistance caused by the deformation of the tyre in contact with the road surface. As the tyre rolls, tread enters the contact area or footprint and is deformed flat to conform to the road or ground. The energy required to make the deformation depends on the inflation pressure, rotating speed and, in some cases, the type of terrain. Understanding rolling resistance and its contribution to a 4x4's off-road capabilities plays a big part in off-road driving.

Tread patterns can vary from mud and snow through to extreme mud (or MT) tyres. These tyres often have stiffer sidewalls for greater resistance against punctures from sharp objects when travelling off-road; the tread pattern is also wider to remove mud from the tread. Many tyres in the all-terrain category are designed primarily for on-road use, particularly all-terrain tyres that were originally sold with the vehicle.

Tread lugs provide the contact surface necessary to provide traction. As the tread lug enters the road contact area, or footprint, it is compressed. As it rotates through the footprint it is deformed circumferentially. As it exits the footprint, it recovers to its original shape. Tread voids provide space for the lug to flex and deform as it enters and exits the footprint. Voids also provide channels for rainwater, mud and snow to be channelled away from the footprint. The void ratio is the void area of the tyre divided by the entire tread area. Low void areas have high contact area and therefore higher traction on roads; high void areas have a low level of contact area, giving good grip in off-road conditions but not so good on damp and wet roads.

A tyre has a code such as:
185/60**R**/15**H**
A/B/C

A = **Width of tyre 9in millimetres)**
In this example it shows the tyre is 185mm wide.

B = **Tyre profile as a percentage of width (A)**
In this example the ratio is 60% of 185mm. This works out as 111mm.

C = **Diameter of inner rim (in inches)**
In this example it shows that the rim is 15" in diameter.

RIGHT The alphanumeric code on your tyre sidewall denotes its width, height and wheel fitment.

Tread lugs often feature small narrow voids, or sipes, that improve the flexibility of the lug to deform as it traverses the footprint area. This reduces stress in the lug and reduces heat build-up.

Fitting the biggest, most aggressive tyre your vehicle will take isn't usually the correct move, as having too much traction can put more strain on differentials, half-shafts and other transmission components. Sometimes it's good for a tyre to be able to spin or unwind in order to relieve any transmission wind-up that's occurring. Also, when fitting oversized tyres make sure you account for axle articulation. Will the tyre fit under the wheel arch when the suspension is compressed? It sounds obvious, but it's surprising how many naive off-roaders make this elementary mistake when 'upgrading' their 4x4.

Ply rating

This term describes the strength of a tyre's casing, which comes in different strengths; for example, some can be a 6-ply rating while others are 2-ply rating. It originated back when tyre fabric was made of cotton, which was the only material available at the time that would stick to rubber once it had been vulcanised. In order to contain air pressure within the tyre, two or more layers of this 'rubberised' fabric were used on the bias or sidewall, in a cross-like fashion. In order to cope with vehicle loads and increased speeds, more and more layers were added to allow the tyre to be used at a higher pressure. However, eventually (due to the increasing number of layers) the tyres became so bulky that they would overheat and explode.

As technology developed and stronger synthetic fibres such as nylon and polyester were introduced, less fabric had to be used for each tyre to achieve the same casing strengths. Consequently an 8-ply rating tyre may only have had four layers of fabric (piles) but would have the same *strength* as eight piles of cotton.

Why is ply rating important for an off-road vehicle? Because many punctures are caused by sidewall damage, so having a stronger sidewall will obviously increase resistance to puncture and sidewall damage. This sidewall strength also helps when you decide to reduce tyre pressure for certain terrain. Lowering tyre pressure increases the footprint of the tyre

LEFT Lowering tyre pressures provides a greater 'footprint' in sand.

in contact with the surface, but obviously a bulging sidewall is more susceptible to damage, so a higher ply-rated sidewall will help.

Years ago a good off-road tyre was something with a- 6 to 8-ply rating. But as technology continued to progress many tyre manufacturers abandoned the term 'ply rating' as they felt it was misleading for the consumer. The term 'service index' is now more popularly used, which uses a coded system of speed and load to determine the load a tyre can bear at a maximum specified pressure and speed. This service index appears on the tyre sidewall after the size branding, but a ply rating can still be seen on many 4x4 tyres.

Greenlaning

Standard tyres will cope in most situations, but an all-terrain type with a high ply rating on

BELOW LEFT An original-equipment 'all-road' tyre tread pattern.

BELOW RIGHT A mild 'all-terrain' tread pattern.

RIGHT An aggressive-pattern mud tyre.

RIGHT The less-aggressive tread of this modern all-terrain pattern is still capable of dealing with mud and snow.

the sidewalls will be a more versatile performer and avoid damage if there are sharp stones concealed in the ruts. Try to avoid aggressive mud tyres because of the damage they can cause to the surface of the track.

Off-road sites

We recommend all-terrain tyres to get you through most of the challenges you'll face, although for really serious mud-plugging you may decide to opt for mud tyres. You may also choose them because they look the part, of course…

Driving abroad

Try to run standard wheels and tyres when you're abroad, as they'll be easier to replace if one gets badly damaged. Fitting oversized, non-standard sizes can leave you stranded in the middle of Africa, which can be inconvenient at best and, in a worst-case scenario, life-threatening.

Run standard steel wheels abroad because they can be knocked back into shape with a hammer if they get damaged on a boulder. A damaged alloy wheel, on the other hand, cannot.

Standard road-biased tyres are the perfect choice for long overland trips – for example

across France and Spain to Morocco – because they make the long motorway miles through France and Spain a more comfortable experience (and achieve better mpg) while they're perfect in the sand when you finally arrive in the desert, because they don't dig in as readily as more aggressive tread types.

Don't ever be tempted to fit an odd size or type to one wheel even in an emergency, because doing this over even a short distance will cause severe transmission damage to your vehicle – and if that happens you'll really be stuck. Needless to say, it's also illegal and very dangerous.

Snow and ice

In places like Scandinavia and the French, Austrian and Italian Alps, which experience severe winters, special ice tyres with metal studs, or snow chains that can be fitted to standard tyres, are often a legal requirement. They certainly give you grip in conditions where ordinary rubber would be hopeless.

The downside is that studded tyres are expensive and it's an uncomfortable and dirty job fitting snow chains to your wheels while crawling around in the snow. But that's the price you pay if you want to drive in these extreme conditions.

If you do decide to travel abroad to experience snow driving, make sure you choose snow chains with a diamond pattern rather than ladder pattern, as these offer better sideways grip if you get into a slide.

Extreme

While extreme tyres with very aggressive tread patterns aren't great all-rounders (because their road manners can't be so good with less rubber in contact with the road), they're immensely popular for very tough off-road applications, like challenge events. If you're thinking of taking part in gruelling contests in the UK, or even far-flung jungle adventures like the Malaysian Rainforest Challenge, this type of tyre is what you need.

But as we've already mentioned, the sheer grip these tyres can achieve in deep mud and the like will put tremendous strain on your transmission system. Drivers of competition-prepared off-road machines will usually fit heavy-duty half-shafts and upgraded diffs to help prevent breakages – although some will still occur, especially when the transmission receives the immense shock of a fast-spinning wheel suddenly finding grip.

Best of both worlds

As you'll have realised, there's a great choice of tyre types for the 4x4 owner, with varying characteristics. Mud tyres will never be so good on the road as road tyres, and vice versa, but you can get the best of both worlds by running your vehicle on two sets of wheels of tyres … your standard wheels and tyres for everyday use and another set of wheels shod with mud tyres for weekend off-road sessions. Many suppliers will now offer good deals on a set of steel wheels, so it's a sensible option. And it's always a good idea to talk to the suppliers who advertise in specialist magazines, as they'll be able to offer you great advice on the sort of tyres that suit your vehicle and your off-road requirements.

Tyre damage

Damage to your tyres can prove extremely dangerous. It can lead to a flat tyre, or even a blowout. The flat tyre will leave you with the inconvenience of having to change the wheel at the roadside, but a blowout at speed could cause a major accident, as sudden deflation of the tyre can cause the vehicle to spin out of control. You can imagine the consequences of this occurring while driving down a busy motorway or dual carriageway at speed.

When you go off-road driving, check your tyres on a regular basis. Damage can be caused by many different things, including pot holes, sharp rocks, flints, thorns and aggressive spinning of the wheels on high-friction surfaces. Another common cause of tyre damage is hitting rocks and even kerbs with the sidewalls. This can cause deep cuts to the sidewall of the tyre, which is its main strengthening structure.

Make sure when checking your tyres that you look at the sidewalls carefully to see if there are any splits or cracks. If there are you should replace the tyre straight away. Checking tyre pressure is also a critical part of your tyre checks. This is especially important on 4x4 tyres because if they're under-inflated they'll heat up and this could also cause a blowout.

Some signs of tyre damage will become apparent when driving the vehicle. If the steering wheel vibrates this could mean that the tyres have a flat spot or the tyre has become misshapen. A flat spot on a tyre is caused when a vehicle brakes hard and skids; this part of the tyre may then become slightly flatter than the rest.

Steering wheel vibration can also be caused by the loss of the weights fitted to balance a wheel, or mud stuck to the tyre rims, so make sure you check for this before going back on to the road. Removing lumps of dried mud from the rims can often cure a wobble that's been diagnosed as something more serious, like a wheel bearing or ball joint failure.

ABOVE Modern wider tyres do not dig into the surface to find grip as effectively as narrower tyres.

LEFT Check tyre pressures regularly.

Chapter Five

Types of terrain

OPPOSITE Another fine mess… but your 4x4 can get you out of it if you understand the terrain characteristics and the use of momentum.

ABOVE Muddy water
is most likely to be
encountered on farm
and forest tracks, or
when green-laning.

Thick forest, dense jungle, open plains, barren tundra, saturated peat bog, treacherous swamp, powerful rivers, precipitous mountains, sandy desert, rocky desert, sand dunes, steep hills, paved roads, thick mud, deep snow and dusty dirt roads are just some of the different types of terrain you can encounter around the world.

Many of these are dealt with elsewhere in this book, but for the purposes of this chapter we'll deal with the sort of terrain you're likely to encounter closer to home, in Britain and Europe. Mud and ruts… sand and gravel… wet grass… snow and ice… they're all out there waiting to claim another off-road victim.

Mud

Off-roaders can expect to encounter a lot of mud. It's amazing stuff that varies in its consistency from one part of the country to another – sometimes from one corner of an off-road site to another – but what it all has in common is its ability to get unwary drivers hopelessly stuck. In this respect heavy, claggy, clay-type mud is the worst. But even light, loamy or sandy mud can be a challenge.

As with most off-road driving techniques, it's crucial to understand resistance and how to overcome it. It'll come as no surprise that mud offers a greater resistance than most other ground types you're likely to encounter.

So what is mud? Well, it isn't just sticky goo. It's amazing stuff. In fact our lives depend upon it.

Mud, of course, is wet soil. And without soil, wet or dry, we wouldn't be here. Everything on the planet relies upon soil for its existence – even the creatures in the oceans (the seabed is, after all, just very wet mud).

Mud – or rather soil – is an intricate mixture of components that ensure life on this planet. The main constituents are ground-up minerals

eyes more effectively. Not only should you be aware of road ice and other slippery conditions, but you should also double the distance you normally allow between you and the car in front. Look ahead and get ready for corners and other obstacles before you arrive at them. A good driver looks ahead and anticipates problems, while an inattentive driver doesn't watch the road and is forced to react to problems, usually abruptly and sometimes disastrously.

Brake before you enter a corner: smoothly apply your brakes before you reach the corner and then release the brakes and use all the grip of the car to corner. Then, once you're through the turn, accelerate out. If you do need to brake, apply gentle cadence braking, which means lots of short, sharp applications of the brake pedal in rapid sequence. Under no circumstances stamp on the brake pedal, or you and your 4x4 will most likely do a striking impersonation of Bambi on ice.

Always avoid travelling too close to the vehicle in front.

Make sure you carry recovery and survival equipment in the vehicle, even if you're just travelling a few miles to the nearest town. A shovel could help you dig your way out of a snowdrift, and some old matting or hessian sacks could give you grip under spinning wheels when all else fails.

If you do get stuck and/or your engine packs up, you'll soon find out for yourself that even the inside of your vehicle can be a very cold and inhospitable place. So carry blankets, a flask of hot drink and some food. It could save your life.

So, to recap: when driving snow and ice, slow down and read the road to choose the appropriate speed. Remember that slippery roads make every mistake happen faster and more dramatically. Mastering control of your vehicle in snow and other winter driving conditions comes with learning proper driving techniques and with experience. In time you should develop what Vince calls a good 'seat of the pants' feel for winter driving, meaning an intuition about how your car will behave in certain situations and circumstances.

ABOVE Caution is the watch-word when driving on ice and snow.

BELOW In severe weather like this, your braking distance will be increased, so always keep a safe distance from other vehicles.

Chapter Six

Top ten off-road problems

OPPOSITE An avoidable problem – the driver has not read the terrain correctly, and is spinning the wheels unecessarily searching for traction.

steep hill, for example, ask yourself if you're experienced enough to take it on. If you don't know the site or green lane, and you're suddenly confronted by an unknown obstacle like a blind hill or deep water, get out and check it out on foot before committing yourself to driving it.

Don't be afraid to ask for advice if there is someone experienced around. At most venues there are areas suitable for novices who don't want to risk damaging their vehicles – and the same applies with green lanes: there are some that are basically hard-packed tracks offering no challenge, but will all add to your experience. Always drive within your own and your vehicle's capabilities. Never drive too fast and never show off to your mates.

Explore a new site by engaging first gear, low box, and letting the vehicle travel around at tickover speed while you get to know the lie of the land.

2 Be prepared

Always carry a proper recovery rope and shackles and make sure you know where the front and rear recovery points are on your vehicle. If you get stuck, beware of being towed out by the rear tow hitch – it's not unknown for the rope to slip off the ball. Always make sure it's properly secure. Tell people where you're going (get OS maps for the area) and roughly what time to expect you back; if you're off greenlaning we recommend going with a friend or two – and remember that in remote areas mobile phones may not work. Carry water and some snacks, have at least a spade and a machete or axe on board, but be careful what you chop down (be friendly to the environment) and who's standing close by when you're swinging your chopper around. Make sure you have enough fuel for the trip and that all your fluid levels are checked; check tyres and the spare, carry a few tools and some get-you-home remedies like tank tape, Radweld, instant metal. Motor vehicles can be dangerous, even if they're travelling slowly around an off-road course or meandering down a green lane, so make sure everything inside the vehicle is securely fastened, including its occupants. Everybody should be wearing seat belts. Don't

ABOVE If in doubt, check it out! A little time spent checking the route ahead will ensure that nasty surprises are avoided.

BELOW Ensure that recovery equipment is securely attached, and adequately rated for the job in hand.

1 Look before you leap

Look and risk-assess: too many times we see novice drivers blindly follow other vehicles and tracks with no idea of the capability of the vehicle in front, nor the driver's experience. When you arrive on a 4x4 site or an unknown green lane, climb some high ground if possible and take a look around. Note where the hills, mud and water are, look for any obstacles. Observe other drivers taking on the challenges. If you see them getting into trouble on a

let anybody hang out of the windows; in fact you should only have the windows open about an inch when travelling along. And don't use an off-road driving day as an excuse to let your kids have a go at the wheel. This is no place for inexperienced or under-aged drivers.

3 Insurance and legality

Did you know that the insurance on your car is unlikely to cover you for damage caused on an off-road site, both to you and your vehicle and to other people's property? A reputable off-road site will carry third party insurance cover, but this won't cover your vehicle; most will make you sign a disclaimer that makes you aware that you're using the site under your own guidance and that you're aware that it's a dangerous location where incidents and accidents can happen, as it's private property.

You should also consider contacting your insurers and updating your policy if necessary.

PS: When you're out greenlaning, remember that byways are legal public highways, so your car insurance should cover you – but check. And since it's a legal highway the same rules that apply on a road also apply on a green lane; so drive sensibly and keep within the law.

4 Read the ground

Always watch what's ahead of you. Before you drive up or down a steep hill, make sure you're lined up properly and that your front wheels are pointing straight ahead. If you do fail to ascend a steep hill, or the ground is too slippery, always adhere to the correct procedure for a failed hill climb – never allow your vehicle to roll back out of gear, or feather the brakes, in case you go out of control and roll over. You need to understand the approach, departure and ramp breakover angles of your vehicle. These are points which will cause either the front, rear or underside of your vehicle to get grounded if you're tackling a particularly severe slope. Long-wheelbase vehicles like Land Rover Defender 110s are particularly susceptible, and if you're not careful you could end up damaging your rear tow hitch or lower bodywork.

5 Don't get cross, get even

Driving over potholed ground looks pretty easy in a 4x4, with its high ground clearance, but beware of getting cross-axled. This is where the sequence of holes puts one front wheel in a deep depression at the same time as the

LEFT Bridles must be used to spread the load on some vehicle-recovery or lash-down points.

rear wheel on the opposite side of the vehicle. If neither of those wheels gets proper traction they'll spin aimlessly, regardless of whether you've got the centre diff engaged or not.

How do you avoid this? Look at the ground in front of you and remember what we told you earlier how your 4x4 system works. Look at the ground ahead, try to find the route of least resistance and try to keep both axles level, which will keep the downforce to each individual wheel about even.

6 Water, water everywhere

There's no better vehicle for tackling water than a 4x4 with its higher bodywork, slightly higher air intake and powerful engine which enables you to push through deep water; but you have to understand wading techniques. For starters, don't go surging in at high speed, sending water flying everywhere and possibly driving into even deeper water where recovery is difficult and you wreck your engine; you could also

ABOVE Enter water slowly, and build up speed gradually.

BELOW A gentle 'bow wave' will be formed when wading at the correct speed.

end up doing serious damage to your vehicle's electrics and taking water into the axles and gearbox ... and, more importantly, endangering you and your passengers.

First, watch other vehicles through the water section; if no other vehicles are around then you'll have to wade in and check for obstacles and the depth. Drive at a steady speed, sending a bow wave ahead of the car, then drive at a speed that keeps that bow wave at the same distance ahead of you. The depression which follows the wave will keep the water out the engine compartment and away from door seals – provided the water isn't too deep.

7 Stuck in a rut?

One of the mistakes a first-time off-roader is certain to make is when he or she tackles deep ruts. Once your wheels have dropped into them and the ruts are deeper than your maximum ground clearance, you won't get out, no matter how much you wrench the steering wheel.

In fact don't turn the steering wheel at all, or you could end up a real cropper and even damage the steering. In reality this should never happen because you should have seen the telltale signs and walked the section first. But sometimes we have to use momentum to carry us through the deeper ruts and, of course, this can help us clear one section; but because we can feel the underside of the car making contact with the ground we daren't lift off to the throttle because the increased drag will bring us to a stop! Look for areas on the raised parts between the ruts, which may or may not be scraped down to the mud or rubbed smooth by the passage of other vehicles. We've already mentioned these scrapes, or 'witness marks', in an earlier chapter. They'll give you a good indication that there could be a problem; but of course, you won't know the type of vehicle that made them, its ground clearance or its speed etc, so you won't know how badly these ruts will affect your own vehicle.

BELOW As your experience develops, you will be able to read the ground from both inside and outside the vehicle.

RIGHT A classic example of a 4x4 driver travelling down deep ruts with his front wheels on lock – dangerous when he exits the ruts and suddenly lurches to the left.

8 Steering

So often we've seen drivers travelling along in ruts with their front wheels on lock. Besides exposing the sidewalls to damage from rocks and sharp stones, it also means that when the vehicle reaches an area where the side walls of the ruts are softer or lower than where you've been travelling, then the tyres could find grip, climb, and will suddenly slew the vehicle sideways in the direction the wheels are pointing. This can cause very nasty accidents, by putting you into trees, ditches and other vehicle, so beware!

9 Failed hill climbs

Too many times we stand watching the driving at off-road sites wondering in amazement when we see vehicles hurtling backwards out of control having failed a hill. The speed a vehicle can come backwards down a hill is frightening and can cause serious damage to occupants if it rolls over, or to other vehicles and watching crowds should it hit them. So before you attempt a steep hill, mentally go through the sequence of what you must do if all goes horribly wrong. Remember, don't depress

OPPOSITE Momentum can overcome loss of traction in cross-axle situations.

the clutch and don't put the handbrake on – it's a parking brake. Make sure your wheels are straight if you start to slide backwards, and go through the failed hill climb recovery technique (see chapter 8).

10 Before you leave...

Before going back on the road, check: are the tyres OK? Make sure you haven't caused damage that could lead to a blowout at high speed on the way home. Check the sidewalls and for signs of a puncture.

Clean off the mud. If possible, drive through water a few times to get the worst of the muck off the underside and the wheels (mud stuck on the rims will make the wheels appear unbalanced, which you'll feel as vibrations through the steering wheel).

Get a cloth and wash any mud and grime from your lights, windows and number plates. This is a legal requirement, by the way. Ignore it and you could feel the long arm of the law.

Finally, be aware that if you have off-road tyres fitted the treads could be full of mud and small stones; if you travel at speed as soon as you leave the site any vehicle behind you will be showered with mud and small stones.

Chapter Ten

Sand and rocks

OPPOSITE Driving dunes and desert sand requires learning a whole new skills set.

ABOVE Desert sand is not to be confused with beach sand, which is usually firm enough to take a vehicle between high tide mark and 5-6m from the sea.

RIGHT When driving on sand, it is not always a good idea to follow in the wheeltracks of previous vehicles.

We love sand – especially desert driving. Vince, the survivor of countless Sahara expeditions, says it's the most fun you'll ever have off-road in your 4x4 … providing you do it correctly.

Sand covers only about 20% of the Earth's deserts. Most of the sand is in sand sheets and sand seas – vast regions of undulating dunes like ocean waves 'frozen' in an instant of time.

Don't confuse desert sand with beach sand, which is usually firm enough to take a vehicle between high tide mark and 5–6m from the sea. Beware of incoming tide and the suction – if you sink just a little bit it will bring you to a halt, and with an incoming tide washing around your wheels your vehicle will be going nowhere. So keep off wet sand, which can contain areas of 'floating' sand or quicksand.

In the case of sand, risk assessment isn't always possible, for obvious reasons. After all, you could hardly be expected to get out of your Land Rover and walk ahead first before driving across the Sahara Desert. It's also difficult to employ ground-reading skills in sand, as soft sand looks much the same as firm sand. It also

Ruts and uneven ground

OPPOSITE The extreme articulation on this Defender is caused by previous vehicles getting stuck and spinning the wheels unecessarily.

RIGHT Deep ruts can hide axle-twisters.

ABOVE Never cross obstacles straight-on, as shown here – always approach at an angle.

BELOW Risk assessment – can I go this way, or shall I find another route?

BELOW RIGHT A little time spent filling in deep holes can make life easier.

Ruts

The easiest way to get your off-roader stuck is to attempt to drive deep ruts. Remember that the lowest points of most 4x4s are the front and rear diff casings or independent suspension arms – usually between seven and ten inches (180–250mm) from the ground – and you'll understand why dropping your wheels into ruts deeper than that will see your vehicle grounded. Although we're talking of ruts as an obstacle to be faced when off-roading, the truth is that they aren't a bad thing. For example, they keep you on the right track and prevent you from sliding into objects like trees.

Once your wheels are down in the ruts, how much clearance is there between your diffs and the ridge between the ruts? Vehicles might scrape their suspension parts, exhaust, bodywork – in fact many contact points beneath a 4x4 vehicle with low ground clearance could make contact.

Ruts can be your best friend or worst enemy. On the plus side, in slippery conditions these grooves in the ground can keep you on track as surely as a Scalextric car. The downside is the balance between the depth of the ruts and the ground clearance on your Land Rover. If the former is greater than the latter, you'll get stuck.

You'll also need to know how to drive across ruts, because if you get it wrong you can damage your steering geometry.

As always, get out of your vehicle and walk ahead to risk-assess the situation. Look at the depth of the ruts and search for telltale signs

Ditch crossings and deep V-shaped gullies

OPPOSITE Deep V-shaped gullies like this one present a unique challenge.

RIGHT A 'V-shaped' gulley does not always have to be V-shaped!

BELOW Washouts resulting in gullies are technically challenging.

Ditches

One of the most amazing features of four-wheel drive vehicles is their ability to cross deep ditches. With diff lock engaged and only one wheel over the ditch (and not in contact with the ground) at any stage, you can ease yourself over what appears to be an impassable challenge.

They may look innocuous, but ditches and gullies cause more people to get stuck and damage the panels of their 4x4s than all the other hazards added together. And the sad thing about that is that they wouldn't have any problems if they tackled the challenge correctly – which is what we intend to explain now...

When you take in the view across a typical off-road site you see big hills, deep water and piles of rocks. They're the obvious hazards, but they're not the biggest cause of damage to your vehicle – that dubious honour goes to ditches and gullies, which can be found anywhere in the world, including deserts and mountains in Morocco, Tunisia, Spain and France. Some are caused by water and wind erosion over millions of years while others are man-made or formed by movement of the ground, including landslides and earthquakes.

As always, you need to get out of your vehicle and risk-assess the situation before you attempt to cross a ditch or gully. How wide is it? Are the sides steep and firm, or soft and boggy?

Ditches and gullies vary a lot, but there's one golden rule for crossing them which should never be broken – and that's never to cross them at right angles. Doing so is what causes you to get stuck or damage your vehicle as you nose-dive the front end into the bottom, foul the rear overhang on the way out or simply get cross-axled halfway across. So first check your approach, departure and overhang – otherwise known as ramp breakover – angles.

The correct method is to try and set the car at an angle of approximately 45° to the ditch or gully. This depends on the width of the obstacle and the wheelbase of your 4x4. The aim is to ensure there's never more than one wheel not making contact with the ground as you drive across. This way you'll avoid getting cross-axled and will be able to maintain momentum throughout the manoeuvre.

LEFT Ditches and gullies can result in approach angles being exceeded,...

LEFT ...the body and chassis coming into contact with the terrain,...

BELOW ...and extreme articulation occurring.

The width of the ditch will affect the amount of throttle you'll need to apply. You may need plenty of momentum to keep you moving, as you're both pushing and pulling your vehicle over and across the ditch. If you're using this technique to drive across deep ruts (which are, in effect, parallel 'ditches') remember that just as your front wheel is clearing one rut, your rear wheel will be dropping into another. So you will need plenty of power to keep the momentum and avoid the risk of stalling and getting stuck.

Because of the resistance, whenever a front wheel makes contact and begins to gain traction it's worth remembering to hold the steering wheel firmly with both hands, keeping your thumbs out of the steering wheel just in case you get some kickback. This is most likely to happen on older 4x4s like 1960s and '70s Series Land Rovers, which lack power steering.

Obviously, the longer the wheelbase of your vehicle the greater the width of ditch you can drive across. Ditches about 4ft (1.2m) wide can be tackled by most 4x4s, but ensure that your points both of approach and departure are free of obstacles and enjoy good traction.

Don't attempt to cross at too acute an angle, or you risk rolling your vehicle. About 6ft (1.8m) is the maximum we'd consider attempting to cross in this way. Beyond that you'll need to build a bridge.

To attempt a ditch crossing, approach the ditch in first or second gear (low box) with diff lock engaged, at an angle of between 30° and 45°. But you must avoid getting cross-axled, which, with a Land Rover and similar 4x4s with the same mechanical arrangement that have a centre-locking diff, means making sure that there are never two diagonally-opposite wheels not in contact with the ground at any time – unless you have axle diff lockers (Mercedes G Wagen and Toyota Land Cruiser) or traction control.

If you're driving a modern Land Rover or other 4x4 with Terrain Response-style traction aid fitted, dial in 'Mud and Ruts', which lifts the suspension, and select low box/first gear where possible.

With a Defender, Classic Range Rover or Discovery 1, select diff lock, low box and first gear.

With a P38 Range Rover, select low box and first gear.

With a Freelander 1, select first gear, with a Discovery 2 select low box and engage diff lock (where fitted), low box and first gear.

With a Series Land Rover, select low box, engage four-wheel drive and freewheeling hubs (where fitted), and use first gear.

Deep V-gullies

Halfway between a ditch crossing and a river crossing, these obstacles can be as challenging as both – and require special skills.

A deep V-gulley is exactly what its name suggests. It's too wide to tackle at an angle, as you would a deep ditch, yet is too narrow to be driven like a conventional river crossing. Deep water isn't likely to be a problem here, but those steep banks are likely to cause you problems with your approach, departure and ramp breakover angles. The longer the wheelbase and the greater the overhangs on your vehicle, the more difficult it's likely to be.

Deep V-gullies are in effect sharp ridges in reverse, and create the same difficulties. They certainly catch plenty of drivers unawares!

You'll occasionally find deep V-shaped gullies on green lanes when you're out in the countryside – we can think of two in the space of a few hundred yards on one byway in Wales – but the place you're most likely to encounter them is at an off-road course.

Before you tackle any deep gully, safely park your vehicle and check it out on foot. Pay particular attention to the sharp ridges at the top of the bank, on both sides of the gully. Are they so sharp that they'll cause you to ground your vehicle? This is most likely to happen on

TOP TIPS

■ Never try to tackle a ditch or gully head-on or you'll come a cropper and nosedive into either the bottom or the far side, depending on the width of the obstacle. You could also get grounded on the edge.

■ The idea is to never have more than one wheel off the ground at any one time. If you do lose contact with a second wheel you'll get cross-axled, and won't be going anywhere in a hurry...

■ The other danger from tackling ditches head-on is the risk of getting the rear end grounded – usually on the tow hitch, but the rear panels are also very vulnerable, particularly on rocky ground.

a long-wheelbase vehicle like a Land Rover Defender 110, but a severe lip at the top of the slope could catch out a SWB vehicle too.

Taking care not to slip, check out the gully itself. If the water is muddy or murky, get in and poke around with a stick to check the depth and composition of the bottom. If it's very soft mud or silt, is there a danger of getting stuck? Also look for rocks, which could prove slippery, or stray bits of wood or branches, which could cause damage if flung up into your engine compartment.

Finally, what about the exit slope? Is it too steep? If several vehicles have gone before you it could be very slippery. If in doubt don't attempt it, and look for another crossing place nearby.

In a Series vehicle, select low box and engage four-wheel drive. Ensure freewheeling hubs are engaged (where fitted). Select first gear.

On Defender, Range Rover Classic and Discovery 1, select low box and first gear. Engage diff lock.

On Discovery 2, select low box and first gear, engaging diff lock (where fitted).

On a P38 Range Rover, engage low box and first gear.

On Freelander 1, select first gear and engage Hill Descent Control.

On modern vehicles with Terrain Response, select first gear and engage low box (where fitted). Select 'Mud and Ruts'.

TOP TIPS

☐ Never approach a deep V-gully at an angle – it's very dangerous. On a very severe or slippery slope the staggered wheels could see you sliding out of control and even rolling over.

☐ Both front wheels should arrive at the top of the slope at the same time, which means you won't be going downhill at a dangerous angle and will be able to maintain safe control.

☐ Vince's usual off-road driving maxim – as slow as possible and as fast as necessary – definitely applies here. Ease your 4x4 down the descent, using engine braking to keep the speed down.

☐ With the front wheels at the base of the exit slope, apply power progressively to overcome any slipperiness, and don't ease off the throttle until you've cleared the lip at the top of the slope.

ABOVE LEFT A purpose-built gulley with excellent traction and good approach angles. If only all terrain was as straightforward.

ABOVE When it goes wrong, it can be awkward...

Side slopes

OPPOSITE Severe side slopes can be traversed with care, but
the surface you're driving will determine how much traction
you can achieve, and the vehicle's centre of gravity also plays
an important part.

How to drive side slopes

Driving a steep side slope is always the thing that's guaranteed to shock a newcomer to off-roading. It doesn't look that impressive to a spectator on the outside, but once you're inside the vehicle it's a very different experience.

It's also one of the most dangerous operations you can carry out off-road … where you're most at risk of rolling your vehicle if you don't know what you're doing. In fact our advice to inexperienced drivers is to avoid side slopes where possible and find another route.

Manufacturers of 4x4s used to boast about the safe working angles of their vehicles, with their marketing material stating that their models could tackle side slopes of 40° or even 45°. But not any more – not in these litigation-happy times – because they know there are too many indefinable variables involved in driving side slopes.

Driving side slopes is a tricky operation, because all sorts of things have to be taken into account – things like speed, unevenness of the ground, traction available, type of tyres and centre of gravity, for starters. For example, if you have a roof rack and a roof tent fitted, your centre of gravity will be much higher and therefore your vehicle will be more unstable when you drive at a steep angle; the number of people in the vehicle (and their distribution),

heavy and insecure loads etc also need to be taken into account. But the biggest factor, as ever, is the driver.

Before tackling any side slope, get out of the vehicle and make a risk assessment on foot. Look out for undulations and hazards like tree roots and rocks in the ground, and check out the traction available to you – for example, is it wet and slippery grass, loose sand and gravel or dry and firm soil; are there rabbit holes that could collapse; and, most importantly, do you really need to drive it?

Slippery wet grass is the most treacherous surface on a side slope and is always best avoided.

Before driving the side slope, we advise asking your passengers to get out and follow on foot (at a safe distance, of course). Any large items like toolboxes or jacks must be lashed down or otherwise secured so that they don't shift when the vehicle is at an angle.

Select low box, first gear, and inch forward on tickover. The slower the better, as it will give you time to react to what the steering wheel is telling you. Going into a side slope at speed is a definite no-no, not least because of the pendulum effect caused by suspension compression and rebound that can send you sliding out of control and, most likely, tipping your vehicle over sideways.

On a wet, slippery surface you won't be able

RIGHT Check on foot for obstacles which could unbalance the vehicle.

LEFT Mud tyres will provide lattitudinal and longitudinal grip, offering some sideways grip on slippery grass slopes, but on this Defender, the additional weight on the roof will raise the centre of gravity.

LEFT Load security is essential when driving on side slopes.

to drive at a very steep angle as your vehicle is likely to start sliding back down the slope. So, as slowly as possible, progress forwards. If the car starts to slide downhill your instinct will be to correct it by turning the steering in the opposite direction. Don't! Your vehicle is telling you that it can't get traction, so don't fight it. You could put yourself and your vehicle in a dangerous position, because if the scrabbling wheels that are pointing uphill suddenly find grip you'll be out of control, and will most likely roll your vehicle.

Just in case you do get it wrong, keep all windows in the vehicle closed. It's a natural human instinct to put your arm out to protect yourself when in peril, but if you do that through an open window when your car's about to roll you'll end up with a crushed arm.

Your aim should be to maintain a steady, low, constant speed, with the steering as straight ahead as possible at all times, but if possible a small amount of steering should be applied up the hill to counteract the tendency for the wheels to break traction and slide.

Should you lower your tyre pressures? There's no doubt that lowering your tyre pressures will give you a bigger 'footprint' in contact with the ground surface and help grip, but unless you're driving through sand, very soft mud or doing a lot of extreme rock-crawling, it isn't usually necessary. The disadvantages of lowering the pressure include inferior ground clearance and making your sidewalls more susceptible to damage from sharp rocks. The sidewalls will also compress

BELOW Slow and cautious is always the best policy when driving at angles such as this.

more on the downside of the vehicle, which will increase its angle – plus it's very time-consuming to re-inflate your tyres … and failure to do so before you go back on tarmac will adversely affect the vehicle's handling and could cause an accident.

The basics

We're talking about side slopes you could encounter on an off-road site or green lane, or perhaps a mountain track in North Africa when there's been a landslide and you have to manoeuvre around it. Traversing along the side of a hill is *not* what we're talking about, because so many unknown permutations could apply. We recommend you never attempt it, but find another route instead.

You need to drive as slowly as possible, so first gear and low box are essential. Engage the diff locks available (depending on your vehicle) for maximum grip. Remember, with the vehicle leaning over, the weight transference will compress the suspension on the downside of the slope, meaning the upside suspension will be expanding and there'll be less downforce on the two wheels on the higher side of the slope. Less downforce means the diffs could send the drive to the wheels with the least resistance, which isn't what you want when you're already going pale and sweating because your vehicle is seemingly defying gravity!

As you approach the slope, there may be a natural tendency for your vehicle to slide. If it does, avoid the temptation of trying to correct it by steering into the hill, because your vehicle is actually telling you that it can't grip – and shouldn't be argued with. If necessary, steer downhill; if the situation requires a fast response you could even hit the gas. Then, once in a safe position, reassess the situation. To do otherwise is asking for trouble.

Don't try to get out of a vehicle that's leaning over if the door you open is on the downside of the slope, as the weight of the door could be enough to destabilise the vehicle's balance. Likewise, if it all goes wrong and you're in a precarious position make sure helpers don't come to the side which is leaning over, because if the vehicle rolls unexpectedly they could get injured.

TOP TIPS

☐ Get out and risk-assess on foot: look out for tree roots, rocks and other undulations that could throw your vehicle out of balance. Even rabbit holes hidden by long grass could spell disaster!

☐ The aggressive tread patterns of mud tyres (right) will always offer better grip for side slopes than normal road tyres (left). Tyres should be at recommended pressures – do not under-inflate.

LEFT Tyre types compared.

BELOW Vince's expedition-prepared Defender has a high centre of gravity so side slopes should be tackled with caution.

☐ Don't be tempted to compensate for sliding downhill by steering uphill, as this could be enough to tip you over if the wheels that are pointing uphill suddenly find enough traction to give you grip.

☐ Heavy items should be lashed down securely so they don't slide about. Try not to have too much weight on the roof rack, as this could adversely affect your Land Rover's centre of balance.

☐ Side slopes will cause the suspension on the uppermost wheels to compress, while the suspension on the lower wheels will be extended. Stiff suspension is better than soft for side slopes.

☐ Never put your arm out of the window when tackling a side slope because it could get crushed if the vehicle tips over. For that reason, all windows on your Land Rover should be securely closed.

Chapter Fourteen

Wading

OPPOSITE The wading depth of your off-roader can be enhanced by fitting a raised air intake (which is also known as a snorkel). *(Land Rover)*

A perfect bow wave, resulting from the correct gear and speed.

Everybody knows that 4x4s and water were made for each other. Even owners who wouldn't dream of getting their beloved vehicles muddy on an off-road course can't wait to go wading. Most 4x4s can be driven in water that's axle-deep without taking special precautions. When the water is deeper you need to know where your engine's air intake and engine computer are located – and don't allow water to enter and reach either of them!

However, it should be said that river and stream crossings shouldn't be attempted by the novice off-roader, especially deep water crossings. We've seen some very deeply submerged vehicles on pay-and-play sites, so our advice is wherever the water is that you intend to drive in, take care and be cautious. Even those 4x4 vehicles that have been specially modified to wade through water, with raised air intakes and breathers, will have their limitations when crossing through deeper water.

That said, water crossings in a 4x4 can be some of the most exciting and challenging situations you undertake when off-roading, but they can also become expensive when things go wrong. Water can be fatal to an engine. However, the worst-case scenario is that the occupants of the vehicle can themselves be put in serious danger if things don't go as planned. People have died – often by their vehicles getting swept away when the driver has underestimated the depth and power of the current.

So, the first lesson is *never underestimate any water*, and especially the force of flowing water. Water weighs over 8lb a gallon (or about one kilo per litre), and with a typical stream or river flowing at 5–11mph, in a deep river that means a lot of force is being applied to the side of your 4x4. As a vehicle enters deep water it can also become buoyant. Your 4x4's buoyancy depends on how well sealed it is. Basic workhorses like early Land Rovers have rudimentary or non-existent door seals, which means water pours in quickly and prevents it becoming buoyant. Generally speaking, the more modern and upmarket your 4x4, the less likely it is to allow water to leak in. This is good news for your carpets and upholstery, but it can make the vehicle float in deep water. Then it's at the mercy of the water, which could carry it downstream or, worse, roll it over. The latter nightmare scenario is more likely if you have a large load on the roof, making it top-heavy: the higher centre of gravity makes it more susceptible to being rolled over by the water.

In remote corners of the world, like many African countries where there are not many bridges once you leave the populated areas, river crossings are simply concrete roadways laid across the river bed. When it rains, floodwater can travel many miles downstream. It may not be very deep, but the force of floodwater is amazing and Vince has seen fast-flowing water just a few feet deep roll over a fully-laden Land Rover in Morocco. Dave, on the other hand, was once stranded for over 24 hours at a river crossing in Lesotho when floodwater off the surrounding mountains turned what should have been a shallow ford into a raging torrent. There was no turning back, because the river he'd previously crossed was by now also a raging torrent.

The depth to which a vehicle can wade depends greatly on the vehicle itself and whether it has a diesel or a petrol engine. As a rule of thumb, the depth limit of a vehicle is somewhere between the top of the wheel rims and the top of the tyres, but even that is probably too deep for some makes. Check the manufacturer's recommended maximum wading depth.

Diesel engines are best for wading because they don't rely on the petrol engine's HT leads, coil, distributor and spark plugs, which will all suffer when covered in water. If you do have a petrol engine, spray all these components liberally with WD40. But you should still take care to protect the alternator and other electrical items – especially any modules which operate the engine management functions on modern vehicles.

Raised air intakes

Raised air intakes, also known as snorkels, play two important roles. Originally conceived for driving in deserts and other sandy areas around the world, they ensure a cleaner air supply to your engine when driving in dusty conditions. By drawing in air from higher up, less dirt is pulled in with it. This not only saves money, with fewer air filter replacements, it also reduces the risk of engine damage due to heavy dust

BELOW Remember to brake gently once out of the water to dry the brake discs.

ABOVE A well-fitted and sealed raised air intake will help when wading.

deposits. It only takes a small amount of dust to enter your engine to wear it out. A raised air intake also improves your vehicle's wading ability in wet or flooded conditions.

These days the most common reason for fitting a snorkel is to enable the vehicle to pass through deep water, by preventing water from entering the engine via the air filter. Four-wheel drives driven in regions receiving heavy snowfall will benefit from a raised air intake to avoid problems from melting snow.

If you do fit a raised air intake, make sure to regularly inspect/maintain the hoses from the intake to the filter, and likewise from the filter to the intake manifold. If you self-fit a raised air intake, make sure you follow all the instructions; it's very important to make sure that the air filter boxes are sealed (some have holes in the bottom to allow dust and water out), to ensure all hoses are sealed, tightened and in good condition and – most important – to ensure that the join between the snorkel and the existing air intake is properly sealed. If in doubt, get it professionally fitted.

Hydraulic lock

If water gets in, engines can suffer from an 'hydraulic lock'. This happens when the vehicle's speed is excessive, or the air intake is mounted low on the vehicle, when driving through water.

In an internal combustion engine, the cylinder/piston is a closed space. The piston rises in the cylinder, compressing a gas/air mixture into a small space until the spark plug fires; or in a diesel engine the high compression causes ignition, expanding the gas, pushing the piston back on its down stroke. Hydraulic lock occurs when one or more cylinders are filled with water. The piston, trying to rise in the cylinder, makes contact with the water and can't move any further. Water doesn't compress, so it will stop the engine during the compression stroke. If there's sufficient force to turn the engine you'll start breaking or bending parts – especially if the engine was revving high when water was drawn in. The end result is a broken or bent connecting rod, valves or even the engine block.

If you drive a vehicle with a petrol engine and suspect water has got in, remove the spark plugs and crank the engine to eject any water. It's not so easy on a diesel engine, where you need to remove the injectors or heater plugs before you crank the engine over. If you intend to drive it, take out the air filter as this will be soaking wet, and check your engine oil for contamination. With a bit of luck you'll be able to get your engine running, but you should still get it checked over as soon as possible in case internal components have been damaged.

Breathers

Breathers are designed to allow air pressure to equalise when a hot axle or gearbox rapidly cools. This causes the air pressure inside the casing to reduce, which in turn causes air to be drawn in via the breathers. If your breathers are below water level, water could be sucked into them.

Most 4x4 transmissions, axles and transfer cases have breathers, although many are extended into the engine bay and mounted high on the bulkhead. If they aren't extended and you intend to wade then we suggest fitting extensions.

Engine bay

Your engine bay is the primary concern when driving through water. With a petrol engine, getting your ignition system wet will cause the

engine to stall. Not a good thing in the middle of a river, nor that lake on the off-road site you visit. Water on spark plugs, HT leads or the distributor cap, coil or ignition module can all cause an engine to stall. Luckily, though, water on or in the ignition system usually results in just a stalled engine and not actual engine damage. But this can happen in a situation where it isn't easy to dry off your ignition system, such as in the middle of a river or lake. So protecting the important components from water can be the difference between getting across and feeling embarrassed as your car starts to slowly fill with water!

As a preventative measure, you can cover the radiator across the front of the vehicle to minimise water entering the engine bay. You can buy a purpose-designed item for this, but in truth a rubber floor mat, old coat or even a farmer's plastic fertiliser bag (empty!) will do the job just as well. The result is less water entering the engine bay and less water for the radiator fan to spray over the ignition system. It also helps to reduce the chances of water entering the air intake.

To minimise stalling from a wet ignition it's a good idea to spray all ignition system parts with WD40 water repellent before they get wet. Diesel engines usually do better with water crossings since they don't have the ignition system to worry about.

BELOW LEFT A rubber floor mat makes an improvised radiator shield.

BELOW The same job can be done with a plastic sheet or even an old fertiliser sack.

Radiator fan

Inspect your radiator fan. Most 4x4s have a viscous-coupling type fan, which doesn't spin at full speed when the engine is cool and can be a benefit when encountering a water crossing. But you may have a fixed-type fan that always spins at the speed of the engine. To check what type you have, switch off the engine and try turning the fan. If it turns easily with the engine off and there appears to be a clutch mechanism at the centre, this is most likely a viscous-type fan. If the fan doesn't turn easily, or it's definitely the fixed-type, we recommend removing the fan belt before deep wading. The reason is that when a whirling fan encounters water it will flex, and since most engines have little clearance between the radiator and radiator fan, as the fan bends the blades could break, and possibly damage your radiator.

Wading techniques

Prior to a crossing or driving in unfamiliar water you should walk it and carry a long stick to prod around below the surface to determine whether the bottom is soft or hard and to check for submerged obstacles. If you can't walk it and suspect it's unsafe, don't risk driving it.

It's a good idea to have your recovery equipment easily accessible and ready for use, already attached to a recovery point if possible; trying to connect to recovery points and tow bars when a vehicle is submerged is difficult and dangerous. When you do need your recovery equipment you may be in an emergency situation where time is critical. If your recovery equipment is buried beneath other gear, the last thing you want to do is have to hunt for it, especially if you're stuck in a stalled vehicle in the middle of a river crossing.

Before beginning to wade, ensure you've prepared your vehicle. Make sure you're happy with your route and check you have a suitable point on the far side to aim for. Switch off headlights and allow them to cool, as sudden contact with cold water will cause the glass to crack. It's a good idea to take off your seat belt and wind down your window (in case you need to exit the vehicle in an emergency). On some Land Rovers the air intake for the cooling fan is mounted on the wing top: cover it up to prevent water ingress into the fan, which could possibly burn it out.

When entering the water, typically using low range second gear with all traction enhancement devices engaged, and at about 1,100–1,350rpm, accelerate as you enter the water until a bow wave has formed at about 1,500–2,000rpm (about 10–12mph) which creates just about the

BELOW When approaching unfamiliar, virgin water, always check on foot for soft ground and obstacles.

WHAT SETTINGS AND GEARS DO I USE?

- On traditional utility 4x4s like Land Rover Defenders: low box, engage diff lock, second gear.
- On modern SUVs: low box, select 'Mud and Ruts' on Terrain Response dial, second gear.
- On vehicles without a low range gearbox: first gear, select 'Mud and Ruts' if Terrain Response fitted.
- On old Series Land Rovers: low box, second gear, lock freewheeling hubs (where fitted).

The above is a general guide only. As always, check the recommendations of your vehicle's manufacturer.

ABOVE When wading at the correct speed, a gentle bow wave will be formed.

right bow wave depending on the height and shape of the front underside of your vehicle. This bow wave helps to maintain momentum and push water ahead of your engine bay; the aim is to create a small bow wave about one metre in front of the bumper – and to keep it about one metre in front of the bumper by adjusting the speed of the vehicle. Why? Because behind the wave will be a much lower trough, situated conveniently immediately below the engine bay.

RIGHT As deep as you may want to go! This photo shows how a good bow wave pushes the water forward and away from the vehicle.

ABOVE Wading too fast forces water into places it should not go!

RIGHT If you drive too slowly through water, with little momentum, if the water gets deeper it will cause greater resistance which may result in the vehicle getting stuck.

Don't slip the clutch, as this reduces control of the vehicle. Remember, the aim is to create a gentle bow wave – not one you could surf on!

To get the speed just right is tricky. Don't attempt to drive too fast through the water. The idea is not to get across as fast as you can. Too fast will send water over your bonnet and possibly into your intake and up your windscreen, causing you to lose vision. Too slow may flood the engine bay and let water in through poor door seals. Follow this advice and you'll get to the other side with no issues. If you have to stop, slow or reverse, avoid riding the clutch as this may allow water and debris to get between the friction plate and the flywheel. If you start to lose traction it's important not to over-rev the engine, just in case the water is close to your air intake, and to stop you digging yourself in deeper! Back off the accelerator and move the front wheels side to side a little in the hope that they may regain traction; if this doesn't work, and it's possible to do so, engage reverse and get out.

If you stall the engine, put the vehicle in neutral without using the clutch and attempt to restart. If you're lucky and you didn't flood the air intake or soak your electrical components, the engine will fire up. It's normally best to use first gear low range and, with a minimum of clutch usage, try to get moving again. If you find yourself stalled in the middle of a crossing and you can't restart the engine, and depending on the force and depth of the water, our advice is to climb out of your window rather than open the door and flood your interior, including electrical components, seats, gear and carpets (although to be honest not many 4x4s are that well sealed and your car will probably slowly fill with muddy water anyway). The possibility of the latter scenario is an excellent incentive for re-reading the preceding paragraphs and memorising what you have to do to get it right...

When crossing fast-flowing shallow streams, cross at an angle and drive slightly upstream. This presents a smaller surface area to the force of the stream. If it's extremely fast-flowing and more than a couple of feet deep your vehicle could be swept away.

Ease off the accelerator as you approach the other side of the water. The exit point could be

BELOW Failure to check the route can result in unexpected underwater obstacles causing problems!

RIGHT River crossings are fun, but can quickly become treacherous, particularly after heavy rainfall.

BELOW After wading, vehicles will drop water for some distance, causing the ground to become slippery for any following vehicles. *(Land Rover)*

a problem area, particularly if you're at the rear of the queue in a convoy of vehicles, due to the water that pours out of their nooks and crannies as they emerge from the river, which will make the exit wet and slippery – particularly if it's rocky or grassy. So make sure you've got enough momentum to power up that slippery slope.

After crossing water or deep mud, check there isn't a vehicle behind you, then apply your brakes several times to dry them out.

Sometimes in emergency conditions we've attached winch ropes to a solid object on the bank or to another, parked, vehicle, then set the winch on free spool as we've made the crossing. This means we can achieve a speedy self-recovery if anything does go wrong.

Maintenance after water crossings

After making several water crossings – or one or two deep ones – you need to inspect your vehicle's differential oil for water contamination. Even if you have extended differential and gearbox breathers fitted, there's no guarantee that water hasn't entered the units. The best time to check the diff for water is immediately after the crossing, but in reality most of us won't check it until later in the day. To properly inspect it after a crossing, allow a few minutes for the vehicle to cool a bit, then loosen the drain bolt and let out a small amount of oil – or dip in to inspect it. If water is present, it will appear to be milky coloured, indicating that water and oil have emulsified. Driving your vehicle for any distance with water-contaminated gear oil can damage axle and gearbox components. If the contamination is so bad that you have to change it where you are, make sure you have the means to take the old oil back home with you for proper disposal. *Never* dispose of oil into the environment.

Also check other electrical items, such as your electric winch (if fitted). After a water crossing, pull out the winch cable and power it back to allow the generated heat to dry out any wet spots. Winches typically aren't used for extended periods of time, but when they're needed you don't want to discover they've been damaged, or have even seized, due to water exposure.

Water crossings should be taken seriously. Water has the potential to cause expensive damage to your vehicle's engine and drivetrain and serious injury to you and your passengers. But with proper preparation and maintenance, the challenge of wading can be as enjoyable as any other off-road experience.

ABOVE After exiting river or stream crossings, check for debris tangled around brake, steering and suspension components.

TOP TIPS

- Seal your vehicle's heater intake with gaffer tape to prevent water ingress. Carry a can of WD40 at all times to spray electrical components. This is absolutely vital with the HT system on petrol-engined Land Rovers.
- Never attempt a river crossing without first setting off on foot with a wading stick to check the depth of the water and the nature of the riverbed. Feel ahead and to both sides, and assess the strength of the current too.
- Driving too fast looks spectacular for your mates but, just like driving too slow, you won't create a bow-wave and you could end up with water flooding the engine compartment – with the associated problems that can cause.

LEFT WD40 and gaffer tape – both can help to protect areas you want to keep dry. What would we do without them?

Chapter Fifteen

Winching and recovery

OPPOSITE A typical recovery for a stricken vehicle, using a rated strop and shackles attached to the correct parts of the vehicle.

ABOVE **The correct front-wheel angle will assist a towed recovery by offering less resistance.**

As an off-road enthusiast, you're undoubtedly going to get stuck some time. You may have help nearby or you may be completely alone.

Let's start with a safety briefing. If you take nothing else away from this chapter, know this: every time you mount an operation to recover a stuck 4x4, be it by winching, jacking, recovery rope, snatching or whatever, you're playing with a lethal force. The damage caused by equipment failure, or improper operation, can and will maim and kill people. Never underestimate it.

There are several options available when recovering a vehicle and to get the vehicle free. Some require a lot of muscle power while others require more brain power.

In all situations when a vehicle is stuck, you must always assess the conditions and make a careful, educated decision on how to recover it. Often a lot of time is wasted when the first recovery attempt fails due to sloppiness or carelessness. So take your time figuring out your escape route/tactic, pulling direction and anchor points. If you're going to use a winch and anchor points are few, make the best use of those you have; if you damage or destroy the only anchor point you have you'll have an

even bigger problem than you originally started with. As with most low-traction situations, momentum is important, so if you get a vehicle unstuck it must be driven or towed to firm ground in one movement; don't stop until you're sure the terrain is firm.

You can get stuck for all sorts of reasons. It could be that you've lost traction because you're driving across particularly soft or sticky ground … or maybe you've bellied out in very deep ruts, or got cross-axled beyond the limits of your suspension travel.

Either way, you'll need to get out of the no-go situation you've found yourself in. The first thing to do, once you've realised that you're not going anywhere, is to take your foot off the throttle. Don't sit there revving the engine and making the wheels spin, because you'll only dig yourself in deeper.

Engage reverse and try driving out backwards. If that doesn't work you'll have to recover your 4x4.

The art of recovery can come in many forms and can get very deep and technical, but advanced recovery techniques, using electric winches in conjunction with kinetic energy recovery ropes, are beyond the scope of this book as they're very specialised and, in inexperienced hands, lethally dangerous. Instead, we want to focus on the basics of using winches and ropes for recovery. We'll first outline the basic recovery methods that every off-road and green lane enthusiast should know.

Kit

The basic equipment you need is a recovery rope, three or four shackles, a spade and a machete. A Hi-Lift-style farmer's jack can be useful on some models, but isn't essential and won't work with many modern vehicles. However, a trolley jack is useful, so always carry it with you, because you don't know when you'll need it. Buy the best you can afford and ensure that it's officially rated strong enough for the job in hand.

Some of the many dangers involved include:

- Improper selection of gear, without understanding load ratings and safety margins.
- Improper use of gear – pulley blocks, shackles, etc.
- Improper use of wire rope.
- Using a tow rope as a recovery rope.
- Not understanding load ratings.
- Unsafe practices – not keeping the area clear, handling wire rope with bare hands, etc.

Every single piece of equipment used in a recovery operation, from tow hook to shackle, MUST be capable of safely handling the enormous loads that will be imposed. It's no good having a 12,000lb-rated winch with a new half-inch thick wire rope if that wire rope terminates in an underrated hook, or, even less obvious, underrated strops and pulley blocks.

How to recover a stuck 4x4

A winch is very useful if you plan to drive off-road alone. Modern electric winches are reliable and easy to operate (as long as you follow all safety rules). Before fitting one, though, make sure the chassis is sound and able to take the immense forces generated. A winch bumper should be well made and properly mounted. Always ensure you use the recommended

ABOVE The minimum basic recovery equipment that should be carried when driving off-road.

LEFT Damaged straps and ropes should not be used.

LEFT Always check recovery equipment for suitable load rating.

TOP TIPS

Read the ground

To avoid getting stuck, get out of your vehicle and use your ground-reading skills to determine whether you can get through. If there are deep ruts, use your shovel to fill them in and reduce the depth.

Stuck and spinning?

If you do find yourself stuck, don't rev the engine and cause the wheels to spin because you'll just dig yourself in deeper. Try reversing back out the way you came.

Recovery kit

Ropes, straps, shackles and a shovel or spade are essential items for the off-road driver and should be carried with you at all times, as you never know when you're going to need them.

Shackles

All straps and shackles are stamped with an SWL (safe working load) rating. These shackles are rated at 4.75 tonnes. Avoid any recovery equipment which isn't stamped with an SWL.

Attach to tow hitch

Tow hitches are attached directly to the chassis of your 4x4, so are capable of taking the strain of a simple recovery. Slip the webbing loop at the end of the rope over the tow ball or hook.

Bridle attachment

Your vehicle's lashing-down eyes are attached to the chassis, but aren't usually as strong as a tow hitch. Equalise the strain by attaching a bridle to both eyes with shackles.

electrical cable and that all connections are tight and completely rust and oxide-free.

We recommend using an electric winch with a minimum of 8,000lb pulling capacity, loaded with around 25m of cable, either steel or synthetic. And make sure you also carry the proper winching kit, which includes heavy-duty gloves, approved and certified shackles, ground anchors, sledge hammer, tree strops and pulley blocks.

We cannot stress the safety aspect too highly: even among experienced off-roaders, accidents happen … and accidents involving winches can be very nasty indeed. We've witnessed some horrific accidents involving winches, including users losing digits after their hands got trapped in them. Having seen this happen – and heard grown men scream in agony – makes us doubly determined to do everything we can to prevent it happening again.

Remember that an electric winch imposes severe drain on your battery, so you may wish to fit a second, auxiliary battery to your vehicle to power the winch and lights, etc, with a split-charging system.

Older vehicles may be fitted with a capstan-style winch that's powered by the engine via a power take-off (PTO) system. Some are fitted with hydraulic winches, which are powerful and in some respects superior to their electric counterparts. But they're usually heavier and more expensive.

Even if you don't fit a vehicle winch, you can carry a hand-operated Tirfor winch. However, these are almost as expensive as electric winches and nearly as heavy, as well as taking up valuable space in the vehicle.

Your Land Rover probably weighs over two tonnes. If it's stuck in glutinous mud the power needed to extract it will probably be three times its weight – and six tonnes is a lot of strain on equipment.

Basic winching techniques

Your 4x4 is the best vehicle in the world for getting you across challenging off-road terrain, but there will be times when even the toughest four-wheel drive is unable to make further progress under its own steam. And when the tough can no longer get going, a winch becomes invaluable.

It sometimes seems that an electric winch is today's 4x4 must-have fashion accessory, you see so many off-roaders equipped with them. But they're most certainly not toys – they're very dangerous if not treated with the utmost respect.

The vast majority of winches sold today are powered by electric motors, from either the vehicle's battery or an auxiliary higher amp battery. They're measured by the amount of dead weight they can pull. For example, a winch rated at 9,000lb will pull a maximum of

RIGHT Winch cable correctly wound and layered onto the drum.

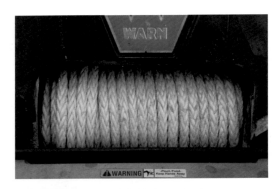

ABOVE A poorly wound and layered cable is susceptible to damage, and may be dangerous.

BELOW Learn and use the correct hand signals.

9,000lb, if the cable on the spool is fully wound out. With more cable on the drum, the power will be more like 4,500lb, so bear that in mind.

As a rough guide, if your winch has 20m of cable/rope on the drum this will probably relate to approximately five layers; for each complete layer on the drum the winch can lose around 1,000lb of pull – many people make the mistake of getting too close to the vehicle they're recovering, or selecting the closest anchor point, and then wonder why the winch stalls. Each successive layer increases the diameter of the drum and reduces the winch capacity to as little as 50% of the rated capacity when the last layer is being wound on the drum.

You have the choice of filling the winch spool with either steel cable or synthetic rope. The former is much cheaper and will last longer, but synthetic rope is lighter and more popular with off-road challenge competitors. The choice is yours. We won't get into which is best, synthetic or wire, but as it happens we both prefer synthetic, as we reckon its plus points, including ease of handling, are greater than wire.

With wire cable it's important that it's spooled on evenly and under consistent tension, otherwise strands of the cable could get trapped and kinked, thus weakening it. This isn't such a problem with synthetic.

For winching you need at least two people. One is the winch operator, who stays inside the vehicle, operating the winch's remote control as well as the vehicle's controls, according to the instructions issued by the winch team leader, who's outside the vehicle directing operations.

Because of the noise of the car engine and winch, it's often virtually impossible to hear what anybody is saying, even if they shout, so the team must agree a clear set of hand signals, which includes when to winch in, when to winch out, fast, slow and STOP! The last is particularly important, which is why we've written it in capital letters. There is an internationally recognised set of winching hand signals. They're easy to find on the Internet: just type 'winch hand signals' into your search engine.

To winch yourself, you need an anchor point, which usually means such natural anchors as

trees, stumps, rocks and roots. Always attach your strap near the ground when using a tree or a stump as an anchor. You should tie the first tree or stump to a second one to provide added support for the strap if the tree is soft or thin. When using a rock as an anchor, be sure it's large and firmly embedded in the ground, and make sure the attachment doesn't slip under or over the rack – and protect the bark by using a tree strop. You can also use the recovery point of another vehicle – a tow hitch, for example – as a sturdy anchor point. There are also various ground anchors available, because there may not be a convenient tree where you're stuck.

You can construct anchors when natural ones aren't available. One of the best types of constructed anchor that can be used for heavy loads is called a 'deadman anchor'. It consists of a log, or your spare tyre, buried in the ground with the winch line connected to it at the centre. When digging, slant the hole at least 15° from vertical and undercut toward the disabled

ABOVE A well set-up recovery being staged for training.

BELOW Trying to secure a ground anchor can be a challenge.

vehicle. Attach the winch line to the centre of the deadman so that the main or standing part of the line leads from the bottom. Dig a narrow trench for the towline; bear towards the centre of the deadman.

All people observing the operation should stand outside the angle formed by the cable under stress at a distance at least equal to the distance between the two most distant points in the rigging. A snapped winch cable reacts like a whip. It can easily slice trees – and therefore people – in half. A snapped synthetic rope doesn't have the same amount of recoil.

As already mentioned, winching really needs at least two people, but if you do find yourself alone select or construct a strong anchor. Attach a snatch block (if required) to the anchor with a strap. Remember, the purpose of this operation is to recover a vehicle, not to pull out stumps. To do this single-handed you need to put the winch lever into freespool and walk slowly with the wire/rope; if you walk fast and stop suddenly the winch drum could overrun and the cable become very loose, which could cause damage to the cable/rope if the winch is wound in without the loose cable being fed and laid back onto the drum correctly.

Always leave at least three turns of cable/rope on the drum, as this will help it tighten on to the drum and prevent it being pulled off by the winch action.

When spooling the cable or rope back on to the drum it's a good idea to 'tension' it back on by pulling a small load towards the vehicle. Keep your hands away from the winch at all times. Make sure the layers are level and not crossed at any point, and be aware of the winch 'overrun', which is the amount of time a winch continues to spool in or out when the hand control is switched off; this overrun varies from winch to winch – some stop almost immediately while others can carry on for nearly a metre.

Never bend the wire cable at a sharp angle or around a sharp corner like a chassis or spring hanger – the cable will kink, causing a weak spot, and it won't roll on to the drum evenly.

Run the winch cable through the block and back to the vehicle. Lift the bonnet to protect the occupants should the snatch block/cable snap. Check your rigging, always fit any hooks so that the hook is facing upwards; then if it comes unattached or slips off it will fly along the ground and not up in the air. Don't start to winch in until you check every element in your rigging and are satisfied that you made no mistakes. Winches are extremely dangerous, so take care.

Winch carefully. Wear strong leather gloves, as sharp bits of metal cable often stick out and can cause nasty wounds to the hands and legs. Never allow your hands within a metre of a revolving winch drum. Never load the winch if the cable is running criss-cross over the drum or the cable is loose on the drum – this will cause the cable to slip and jam; it may also crush the cable, causing flat spots.

Take up the slack gradually, sit in the vehicle to operate the winch control and pull the vehicle forward with its winch – pressing gently on the accelerator to keep putting charge into the battery will also help. Remember that your electric winch can draw up to six times more current than your alternator can supply, which places extreme demands on your alternator and battery (or batteries). A standard battery can only power a winch under full load for about seven minutes until it's totally flat.

Power may be gently applied to the wheels at the same time as you winch, but don't spin excessively; you need to be careful that your vehicle, or the vehicle being recovered, finds grip and moves forward. If your winch sounds like it's struggling, and where possible, use at least one snatch block, and in tough conditions

BELOW When pulling out the winch cable, make sure that three or four coils are left on the drum to provide bite on the drum and to prevent the cable unwinding completely.

FAR LEFT Pulley blocks can be used to double the mechanical advantage and to divert the direction of pull.

LEFT Ensure that any recovery ropes or straps are properly secured to the vehicle(s).

use two, which ensures the winch and electrical system aren't overloaded or over-stressed. A mechanical advantage is gained by using a snatch block or pulley. A small force, when moved through a long distance by one or more mechanisms (pulleys), will move a large weight (vehicle) for a short distance.

When using a pulley block, you gain a 2:1 mechanical advantage. Attach a snatch block to the vehicle to be recovered or to your anchor point if self-recovering. Next, run your winch cable through the block and secure the cable to the winch vehicle.

The same techniques are used to recover another vehicle, but instead of having to find an anchor point, you connect your winch cable to the stranded vehicle via the hook and a suitable fixing. If you're recovering a vehicle that's well and truly stuck and the winch starts to pull you towards them, you can do several things to counter this, like turn the steering wheel so the vehicle is on full lock to increase resistance, chock the front wheels, or secure the winch vehicle to either another vehicle or a tree to help it hold its ground.

After using the winch, have one person pull back on the cable while it's wound slowly, evenly and tightly back on to the drum, layer by layer.

Shackles

There are two types commonly used in the off-road world: D-shackles and bow shackles. D-shackles are narrow shackles shaped like a loop of chain, usually with a threaded pin closure. They're very common, and most other

ABOVE Be wary of the winch overrun when spooling the cable back onto the drum.

LEFT A typical D-shackle and a bow-shackle.

ABOVE LEFT The high-lift jack located and secured, with the lift operation in progress.

ABOVE Make sure that the jack mechanism is clean and adequately lubricated.

LEFT Stand back, keep your head and body away from the jack handle, and listen for the clicks as the pins drop into place at the top and bottom of each stroke.

BELOW LEFT No matter how much effort is required, NEVER lean over the jack handle...

BELOW ...or position your head over the jack – both are extremely dangerous and could result in serious injury if things go wrong.

shackle types are variations of the D-shackle. The small loop can take high loads primarily in line, but its weakness is side loads, which may twist or bend it. The second and probably the most recommended type is the bow shackle, which has a larger 'horseshoe shape' to its loop. This shackle can take loads from many directions without developing as much side load. However, the larger shape of the loop does reduce its overall strength. Only buy shackles which are rated – they may cost more, but they're well worth it.

Exhaust bag jack

This type of jack is very simple and easy to use, provided it can be placed under part of the vehicle. It's quite effective, especially in sand, where, if necessary, a small area can be dug away to accommodate it. It requires the vehicle's exhaust system to be in good condition, as even a small hole will prevent the bag from inflating. It can also cause rusted or weak areas in exhaust systems to blow out.

Be sure when placing the bag under the vehicle that sharp objects are clear of the bag, to avoid punctures. Once in position, connect the pipe to the vehicle exhaust and start the engine (in neutral). When the wheel is clear, stop the engine and simply fill in the hole or rut with whatever is available, or dig away any sand that has built up.

High-lift jack

The best jack to carry for 4x4s used to be the high-lift type. It can lift virtually any vehicle, and with the aid of chains it can be used as a winch. It's still a useful piece of off-road equipment for those that have a vehicle with box sections front and rear, which the high-lift leg can fit under easily, but with most modern 4x4s it can get a bit close to bodywork, even with some of the accessories you can buy which will attach the jack leg to your towing eye or your wheel.

There are two types of manufactured jacks: the cast and steel, and the all-cast. The all-cast seems to last a bit longer under harder use, although the cast and steel type also lasts for many years. Each jack is fully tested

at the factory. Both jacks have a 7,000lb capacity and will lift, push, pull, hoist and clamp equally well.

A basic list of equipment to carry with the jack when using it as a recovery and lifting tool would be two tree protector straps (8ft x 3in), three ¾in D-shackles, 12ft of ⅜in chain with holding hooks – high grade tensile strength – work gloves, and a board about 18in square with a bolt in the middle that fits the hole in the jack base. The board is so that you don't drive the base of the jack into the mud. There are in addition a few accessories that can make life easier. A bumper adapter is great for holding on to those metal edges

TOP TIPS

The basic are:

☐ Place wheel chocks in front of and behind the tyre not being lifted by the high-lift jack. It's also worth stabilising the vehicle somehow to stop it tipping left or right if the jack or vehicle becomes unbalanced.

☐ Set the high-lift jack base on a firm surface with the large runner facing toward the vehicle's bumper. Push the reversing latch up to place the jack in lift mode.

☐ If the ground is soft, use a base to spread the weight and prevent sinking. A piece of sturdy wood about 18in square – like a section of scaffolding plank – will do the job nicely, although you can buy a special base if you want to look the part.

☐ Stand behind the jack, facing the vehicle. Pull the jack handle toward you to release it from the jack bar. Push the handle toward the ground until your hear the jack 'click.' Pull the handle to its highest position until you hear another click, and repeat until you have the vehicle lifted off the ground. Push the handle firmly toward the jack bar until the clip snaps in place. Place blocking under the vehicle frame to support it while raised.

☐ While holding a load, keep the reversing latch in the up position for safety. When switching the reversing latch to lower the load, do so with the jack handle up and preferably try and kick it rather than use your hand! If you don't, the handle can suddenly pop up and nail you in the face or trap your fingers between the handle and bar.

☐ Remove the blocking from under the vehicle.

☐ Move the reversing lever to the down position. Pull the handle toward you to free it from the jack bar.

☐ Push down on the jack handle. Slowly allow the handle to move up. Push down on the handle when you hear a 'click.' Repeat the up and down movement until the vehicle's wheels are on the ground. When the load gets low, under 150lb, and the handle is up, the jack will release and drop to the bottom of travel.

of bumpers and can be adapted to fit other types of bumpers. The lock rack and bumper mount kit are great to secure the jack on the outside of the vehicle.

When using a jack, hold the handle tight at all times and never lean over it while working. We've seen the jack handle fly up during the upward stoke and smash people in the face. So hold that jack handle tight at all times, when jacking up or down, and when you leave it unattended always leave it down. Keep your head and face clear of the up and down route of the handle.

Using a jack as a basic winch

You can even use the jack as a winch. You simply connect an end of one of the straps to the tow hook, or in your vehicle. The other end of the strap is connected with a D-shackle to the top clamp clevis of the jack. The top clamp clevis should be in straight alignment with the jack, not in its clamping position. The base of the jack is facing away from the vehicle. Place the other strap around a suitable tree or anchor. Use a D-shackle to connect the strap around the tree. Don't put the point of the hook in the link hole. The hook should be made so that the link fits in the hook jaw and will hold the entire load to tensile strength. Run the other end of the chain to the jack. Always use the chain first at the jack tongue, then extend its reach with the wire rope between the chain and the anchor. Don't use a recovery strap in this operation as it'll stretch too much.

With the chain, you can tighten the rigging by 'choking' the chain (shortening it) and connecting the hook to an appropriate link. The chain is looped around the tongue of the jack. Now get the rigging as tight as possible and begin to jack using the handle. Use work gloves and watch your fingers.

The vehicle will begin to move as you jack. Be careful that the high-lift doesn't roll over, and watch the tyres and steering closely, keeping it aligned to where you want to go. Once the jack is all the way to the top, secure the vehicle from rolling back in the hole. Move the jack reversing lever down. Loosen the chain. Choke the chain tight and begin again.

I've found it sometimes takes two or three jack lengths to get a vehicle out.

When using these methods of recovery, take care with lights, body panels and fingers, and don't overstress the equipment.

The hardware you use should exceed the capacity of the jack, so that the jack is always the weakest link. There's a shear pin on the jack that will break (a good reason to carry spare shear pins) if the capacity is exceeded. However, of all the vehicles Vince has extracted over the years, including heavy and fully-laden Land Rover Defender 110 expedition vehicles, he's never sheared the pin.

Use the jack carefully and give it regular maintenance and it will give you many years of great service. Spray some WD40 on it once in a while. If used in mud, hose it off when you get home. Spray some white lithium grease on it and it's good to go.

Sideways recovery

Jacking to recover a vehicle is usually done to get a wheel out of a rut when the vehicle is 'hung up', or to fill in wheel holes in dirt and sand by jacking up the entire end of a vehicle with a high-lift jack; the vehicle can then be pushed sideways to allow it to be moved out of a rut or soft section. This procedure must be performed with no bystanders near the jack, in case it springs out.

Here's the procedure. Jack the vehicle in the middle of either end until both wheels are clear of the ground by at least 300mm. Clear everyone from the jack end of the vehicle and position yourself with the vehicle between you and the jack so that it can't spring out and strike you. Be aware of where the jack may end up and ensure it won't contact any part of the vehicle when it moves.

Proceed to push the jacked end until it topples off the jack. This procedure can be repeated at both ends of the vehicle to 'walk' it sideways.

This procedure has inherent dangers, as the vehicle is very unstable with two wheels off the ground. All bystanders should be well clear of the vehicle, and the person operating the jack should be aware that it may 'pop out' unexpectedly.

Brash mats

We've found that, on occasion, where there were no good anchor points, we've had to lift each corner and build an elevated road bed. This procedure takes time, but you're stuck and going nowhere fast anyway. This usually happens in boggy areas where there are deep ruts and the vehicle is high-centred. Lift each corner up as high as needed, bringing the tyre into the air.

Take the time to gather large rocks and stones to use as a base, then lay brushwood and small branches first in the rut running parallel with it and then a layer at right angles, until your mat is just above the height of the ruts; this will allow for compaction. You can also build a small 'roadway' to help gain momentum when you start to move, five to six feet of road (or longer) for each tyre, going in the direction you want to go. Sometimes it only takes that much of a start to get the vehicle going again.

Once out, go back and repair any damage you've caused to the track before you carry on.

Recovery ropes and strops

This topic can be a minefield, so it's our intention to keep our advice simple – and safe. Normally when a vehicle is stuck off-road, the forces required to overcome the suction and weight of a vehicle weighing over four tonnes can be as much as 9–12 tonnes, so the equipment used and the recovery points must be strong, safe and secure. Don't wrap ropes around bumpers or anywhere there are sharp edges; if you have to use the axle as a recovery point, make sure you don't trap brake pipes.

Don't go to a car accessory shop for your recovery rope! The ropes you see there are normally 'towing ropes' and all they have to do is get over the initial rolling resistance of a vehicle broken down on the road and tow it to a garage or a safe location; use them off-road and with a well-stuck vehicle and they'll break. All straps should be clearly labelled with their load (typical rating of around six tonnes), as well as length, material, date of manufacture etc.

There's a big difference between towing ropes and recovery ropes. The major difference is the material the rope or strap is made from. Polyester

ABOVE **It is acceptable to put the eye of a recovery rope over a tow-ball in light towing or recovery situations.**

LEFT **Do not confuse a recovery rope with a snatch strap.**

ABOVE A bridle should be used on some vehicles to reduce the load acting on the points where recovery ropes can be attached.

the ditch. Pulling from an angle (you may have to get quite close to achieve the desired angle) will help pull and lift the vehicle out of the ditch or ruts.

Before you start the recovery, discuss your plan carefully with the other driver and stick to it, including which gear and engine revs to use. Do whatever you can to reduce the effort needed for the pull – *eg* wheel alignment, removing obstacles, digging out approach ramps. At night other vehicles' lights may be more useful than those of the recovery vehicle. It may require more than one tow manoeuvre and may require two recovery vehicles to be joined together, but if it gets to this point and a winch is available then consider using that!

If the vehicle being towed out can be started then a little power will help the recovery; but spinning the wheels wildly will not. Nobody should be close to, or between, the two vehicles.

Towing is defined as slowly taking up the slack. The limiting factor will be traction – namely the friction between the tyres and the ground. So if you're moving a vehicle that's slightly stuck you connect the vehicles together with the correct location/recovery points, drive slowly forward (you can slip the clutch) until you feel the rope tighten – this is called 'taking up the slack' – then come off the clutch completely and accelerate away. Hopefully both vehicles will move away together; if not the vehicle may need 'recovering' as opposed to being towed.

Recovery is defined as taking up the slack at a reasonable speed. The ground conditions and friction between the tyres and ground aren't such limiting factors as in a towing situation, but obviously you need to position the recovering vehicle where it can get maximum traction. Nylon ropes (strops are OK but have no give in them, so are very harsh on recovery points, especially when snatching; ropes provide a slight 'cushion', reducing the shock loading) have more extension then polyester straps and are more suitable for recovery situations because of the minimal stretch they have, which reduces the shock load on the recovery points.

As towing connects the vehicles together, engage any traction enhancement devices like centre diff-lock, and at the first attempt take up the slack and accelerate moderately away.

ropes are towing straps – they have less stretch in them than nylon and are more suitable for towing straps, tree strops and winch extension straps. Nylon straps are recovery straps.

Know where your recovery points are, make sure you have enough of the correct type of shackle to connect your rope to the recovery point, and make sure that the latter isn't just a lashing-down point. On some modern vehicles you have to remove covers to expose the recovery point; we'd recommend doing this before you start off-road driving. If you're unsure and have two recovery points mounted on each chassis leg, use a bridle to distribute the weight. You should use a long enough bridle that those forces are reduced to minimal levels. Ideally the legs of the bridle should be longer than the distance between the recovery points, so that more force is concentrated along the lines of the chassis than is being used to pull the two recovery points together.

Always buy a rope that's long enough – remember that with shackles and doubling up, you can shorten a rope. You may not be able to get close to the vehicle you're trying to recover, the ground may be boggy or the ruts too deep; most times the further away you are from the vehicle you're recovering, the better and safer it is. Always try to pull in a straight line, although this may not always be possible; when trying to extricate someone from a ditch or ruts you may have to overemphasise the angle you pull at, as pulling in a straight line will just pull them along

If the vehicle doesn't move, don't sit there spinning the wheels – stop, reverse and try again. If you're using a proper recovery rope, it's typically made from nylon and has more elasticity then a polyester strop to cope with the shock loads that can occur in recovering a vehicle in comparison to towing one. If this is the case, the second attempt can be made with some slack in the rope; the towing vehicle accelerates away, the slack is taken up and the shock of the small kinetic recovery style will hopefully dislodge the stuck vehicle and get it moving. If not you could try again, but be careful, as the more force you apply the greater the dangers can become.

Kinetic recovery

Kinetic ropes and straps are dangerous, even in the hands of someone who's experienced at using them. We'll explain what they do and how they work, but wouldn't recommend a novice to try. Basically, under maximum load a kinetic recovery rope (KERR) or strap (KERS) will stretch up to 30%. This stretch helps relieve the jerking action commonly felt during vehicle recovery with normal recovery ropes – effectively reducing the amount of stress put through a vehicle and its occupants, if used gently. However, use it as it's supposed to be used. During vehicle extraction, the kinetic rope or strap stretches and absorbs enormous energy from the pulling vehicle. This energy is then transferred to the stuck vehicle, resulting in an extremely effective and efficient vehicle recovery – it's been likened to a champagne cork coming out of a bottle – but the forces involved are incredible. We've seen bumpers ripped off, chassis pulled apart, tow balls pulled out of the chassis – all of which ended up flying through the air at high speed, ready to hit the recovery vehicle or innocent bystanders.

The vehicle being recovered should have the correct recovery points and be strong, as

BELOW Trying to force yourself out of a near-stuck situation can make matters worse!

RIGHT The first step in a kinetic recovery is to fit a bridle to spread the load placed on the chassis.

RIGHT Layering two metres of kinetic rope on the ground will give the recovering vehicle a chance to reach an acceptable speed.

BELOW Make sure that all recovery equipment is securely attached and up to the job.

BELOW RIGHT The driver of the vehicle being recovered must be prepared for the initial surge once slack is taken up, and ready for action!

POINTS TO REMEMBER WHEN USING KINETIC STRAPS OR ROPES

- Towing points must be checked very carefully for safety – if a snatch strap is to be used on a vehicle, both vehicles should be fitted with two recovery points each, and both points must be used, as a kinetic strap has the ability to pull an entire towing attachment off, fling it straight through a vehicle and out the other side. A human body in between will be destroyed.
- Never use a regular towing strap with a snatch strap as the snatch strap is rated at around 15 tonnes – the towing strap may snap, causing untold damage.
- If either of the vehicles has only one recovery point, either find another one or attach the strap directly to the axle

– make sure the surface is smooth and won't cut the strap.
- Read the instructions: kinetic ropes and straps can only be used a specific number of times. After this they must be discarded. It may seem wasteful to throw away a rope or strap that looks perfectly alright and cost you a small fortune, but remember, if it breaks you could endanger yourself, bystanders and your vehicle.
- Snatch straps can usually be identified by their width; they're two or three times wider than regular tow straps, but check the strap itself to make sure – don't assume it to be a snatch strap just because it's wider.

should the recovering vehicle. All bystanders should be kept well clear.

The KERR or KERS is connected to the stuck vehicle and to the recovery vehicle. The recovery vehicle leaves about 1–2m of slack in the strap and drives away from the stuck vehicle; as the strap/rope tightens up, it begins to stretch, sometimes up to about 30% longer. As the recovery vehicle slows down due to the increasing load, the stuck vehicle usually 'pops' out of its hole – but it then speeds up towards the recovery vehicle as the strap/rope contracts; everything happens rather quickly and both drivers must pay careful attention.

Often only a KERS or 'snatch strap' will free a stuck vehicle – it's especially useful when the entire area is very slippery and no vehicle can keep its grip. It's like a giant elastic band. Everyone has played with an elastic band and found that when it snaps it can be painful, and this is the reason for taking serious precautions when using a snatch strap – its stored kinetic energy is incredible.

Self-recovery

A recovery operation without a winch or second vehicle is entirely possible given enough time, planning and hard work.

The main aim when attempting self-recovery is to remove the obstructions preventing the vehicle from moving. This is done by either digging in front of or behind the wheels and chassis, or by lifting the vehicle up from the surface and filling in underneath or 'throwing the vehicle over' to harder ground. Often the terrain is very soft and the vehicle will tend to sink in if it's driven or shaken too much, therefore you must make every attempt to prepare the surface such that the vehicle has the best chance of getting out on the first attempt; if more work can be done to better your chances, do the work first before attempting to drive out.

TOP TIPS

These are the tools to have in your vehicle to assist in self-recovery:

- High-lift or trolley jack.
- Spade.
- Saw.
- Shovel.
- Sand ladders.
- Axe.
- Ratchet straps.

Chapter Sixteen

Winter driving

OPPOSITE A week earlier, Vince had been driving this Defender across the Sahara Desert. Now he's back to a typical English winter. This proves the diversity and all-round ability of your 4x4.

Driving in the winter is very different than at other times of year. Adverse weather and longer periods of darkness make driving much more hazardous. Sometimes conditions can be extreme, as we've found out over the past few winters in particular, with prolonged periods of heavy snow, frosts and floods. This means that we need to adapt the way we drive on- and off-road.

Winter, of course, is when 4x4 ownership really comes into its own. When tarmac is covered by ice and snow you're in effect driving off-road anyway, and the principles of off-road driving apply. The extreme weather we've experienced in the UK in recent winters has certainly resulted in record sales of 4x4s, but just owning a 4x4 doesn't solve the problems caused by floods, ice and deep snowdrifts. As always, you still need to know how to use that 4WD capability in such conditions.

Remember that although four-wheel-drive vehicles can keep going in slippery conditions, their brakes are no better than an ordinary car, and being heavier they tend to have longer stopping distances – even in good weather. Driving technique is especially important when driving in tough winter conditions: the natural capability of a 4x4 can be dramatically extended when it's used correctly.

Different weather conditions create different hazards throughout the winter and in different areas of the country at different times. A single journey may take us into very different weather, road and traffic conditions, so we need to be prepared for each one.

Even if you're the best driver in the world, there will be times when nature will get the better of you and your progress will be hindered. Whatever method you choose, remember to select the highest practical gear, use the absolute minimum throttle and wiggle the steering for best results...

Making the most of the available traction is key to winter driving. Loss of traction can lead to wheelspin under acceleration, wheel-lock under braking and sideways sliding while cornering. There are now many computer-governed vehicle management systems that can control these actions to a limited extent, but there's no substitute for careful driving. In a modern 4x4 switch your Terrain Response to the 'Snow' setting or 'Winter Driving' mode.

Winter driving rules of thumb

- **High- or low-range gearbox:** Use low for control, high for better road conditions.
- **Gears:** Pull away in a higher gear than normal for extra traction.
- **Suspension:** If air suspension is fitted on your vehicle, you can raise it to prevent grounding in deep snow.
- **Diff lock(s):** Engage when slippery.
- **Speed:** Keep your speed down.
- **Traction control systems:** Keep on.
- Leave more room for braking.
- Keep all driver input gentle.

Preparing your vehicle

Always get up at least ten minutes early to give you time to prepare the car:

- Clear all windows of snow and ice using de-icer and a scraper – don't set off with just a tiny hole cleared in the windscreen.
- Check the roof for snow before you drive – once in motion it can slip down over the windscreen and obscure your view.
- Use a cigarette lighter to warm a key for a frozen lock. Don't breathe on the lock, as the moisture will condense and freeze.
- Besides an ice scraper and de-icer, it's worth carrying a mobile phone with fully-charged battery, a torch, first-aid kit, tow rope, blankets, warm coat and boots, jump leads, snow shovel, warning triangle, an old sack or rug and WD40 water-repellent.
- Plan routes to favour major roads, which are more likely to have been gritted.
- Put safety before punctuality when the bad weather closes in.
- Use dipped headlights.
- Top up washer fluids and antifreeze.
- The night before, lift wipers off the windscreen and set wipers to off.

TOP WINTER TIPS

- If your tyres are making virtually no noise this could be a sign that you're driving on ice.
- If your vehicle skids, depress the clutch and turn the steering wheel into the direction of the skid. When the vehicle straightens steer along the road. Don't brake – it will just lock up your wheels and you'll skid further.
- Stopping distances are ten times longer in ice and snow. Keep your distance...
- Gentle manoeuvres are the key to safe driving.
- Reduce your risk of skidding by reducing your speed. Too much power is often the source of problems in snow and ice.
- Wear comfortable, dry shoes – cumbersome, snow-covered boots will slip on the pedals.
- Select second gear when pulling away, easing your foot off the clutch gently to avoid wheelspin. Pull away and accelerate gently and progressively.
- Try to maintain a constant speed, choosing the most suitable gear in advance to avoid having to change down while climbing a hill.
- When driving downhill, choose third or fourth gear to prevent skidding.
- Always apply brakes gently.
- If you do get stuck, straighten the steering and clear the snow from the wheels. Put a sack or old rug in front of the driving wheels to give the tyres some grip. Once on the move again, try not to stop until you reach firmer ground.
- Always be prepared for understeer and oversteer, and know how to correct them. Understeer is when the car continues straight on despite applying steering lock, while oversteer is when the car tries to spin round due to a lack of traction at the rear.
- A sudden, sharp stab on the brakes can momentarily lock the wheels, causing a build-up of snow in front of them which will help to slow the vehicle down. Needless to say, this is a technique only to be used in an emergency.

ABOVE Always go prepared during the winter months.

Equipment and supplies

Always carry the following in your vehicle when driving in winter:

- Snow shovel/spade.
- Scraper with a brush on one end.
- Tow rope (a recovery rope is better) and shackles or other means of connecting to vehicles.
- Torch (with spare batteries).
- Abrasive material (cat litter, sand, salt, or traction mats).
- Jump leads.
- Warning triangle.
- Brightly-coloured cloth to signal for help.
- Fluorescent jackets for all the vehicle's occupants.

BELOW Ice and snow stuck in the wheels can imbalance the wheels and cause vibration through the steering.

- Flask of hot beverage, snacks.
- Sleeping bags or blankets, warm hats and gloves.
- Mobile phone with charger (cold weather drains batteries a lot quicker than normal).
- Avoid alcohol. It lowers body temperature and will cause you to become drowsy.
- Let someone know your route and timing schedule.

If you get stranded

You may feel helpless, stuck in the snow in a lonely place, but there are things you can do to survive until help reaches you:

- Stay in the vehicle – don't wander off and get lost or frostbitten.
- Run the engine for heat about once every hour, or every half hour in severe cold.
- Clean snow from around the end of the tail pipe to prevent carbon monoxide build-up.
- For extra heat, burn a candle inside a coffee can – but don't place the can on fabric.
- Make sure the vehicle isn't airtight, by opening a window a little.

Winter tyres

Depending on the severity of the conditions, it may be worth considering specialist winter tyres. These vary from a 'mud and snow' (M&S) rating through to studded tyres for icy roads. The latter are worth considering if you're thinking of travelling to Scandinavia in winter – or the Alps or Scottish Highlands, for that matter.

Manufacturers of winter tyres use several methods to increase friction and help maximise control. First, the rubber compounds are usually softer, which allows optimum friction to be reached at lower temperatures. Second, winter tyres usually have small sipes formed into the rubber within a tread block. These provide 'grippy' edges that are especially useful when driving in snow. Third, the tread tends to be wider and deeper, which provides more bite when driving in the snow or on ice.

Winter tyres usually also have an aggressive block-like tread pattern which can help to dig into the snow and provide traction (also useful in muddy conditions). Finally, small studs can be fitted to the tyre and these provide a great deal of benefit when driving in icy conditions, although in some countries they're only permitted in the coldest months as they damage road surfaces. Studded tyres can also increase your braking distance when on a clear dry road.

Snow chains

If you're driving in deeper snow, it might be worth considering using snow chains, or at least having some stored in your car. These are fitted to the driven wheels and can provide dramatic increases in traction. If you do choose to fit snow chains, ensure the manufacturer's instructions are followed carefully or damage to your car could result. And be warned that fitting them to the wheels of your 4x4 in extreme sub-zero conditions involves getting very dirty and cold as you struggle to secure icy chains that 'stick' to your fingers.

Other traffic

Driving in snow is as much about dealing with other road users as looking after your own car, so watch the behaviour of oncoming traffic; you may have to avoid them if they slide towards you, and expect other road users to be unable to stop at junctions.

Cars approaching a narrowing of the road uphill won't want to stop in case they can't start again. Cars approaching downhill, may be unable to stop without skidding.

Try to leave a ten second gap between you and the car in front. This gap allows for increased stopping distances, and gives you time to respond if the car in front has problems. If they stop you may have time and space to steer a different course, or by slowing down you can allow time for the obstruction to clear without having to stop and restart yourself.

If the car behind is too close, find a good place to stop and let them go past. Then you can concentrate on the road ahead.

Beware of ice from lorries. Many have tarpaulins that can fill up with snow and water, which then freezes overnight. When they set off in the morning and get up to speed the bits of flying ice coming off the top can be a real hazard to other road users.

Driving on ice

Unlike snow, ice is often invisible. You have to guess where it might be. Look for reflections in the road surface ahead – what looks like water may be ice. And if you travel a road regularly, be wary of places where water collects on the road and may freeze. Road bridges and flyovers tend to freeze first because they're cooled from below.

One of the first signs of slippery conditions is if the steering becomes lighter to turn. The normal tendency of steering to self-centre when you let go of the wheel becomes less powerful when the front wheels lose their grip. If you're aware of this effect you can feel the reduced

BELOW Falling through frozen water can cause thick ice to damage steering components and the radiator.

ABOVE A winch can help with recovery – both self-recovery and recovery of another vehicle – in wintery conditions.

resistance to your steering wheel movements as the road becomes slippery. Another indication that you may be on ice is if the swishing sound of your tyres on a wet road goes quiet.

Avoid skids by driving gently. Avoid harsh acceleration, hard braking, abrupt downward gear changes or abrupt steering movements. These can all cause a skid.

Finally, although bright sun and a warm wind can quickly thaw ice, it may leave patches in

sheltered areas, so be vigilant wherever walls or trees cast a shadow over the road.

If it all goes wrong...

If despite all your efforts you can't avoid hitting something, remember your car offers you more protection in a head-on crash than a side impact. There's a lot more energy-absorbing metalwork between you and the front bumper, than between you and the outside of the door.

Seatbelts and frontal airbags work much better in a frontal impact, and many cars don't have side-impact airbags. If you slide sideways into a kerb or soft ground your car may roll over, whereas if you hit them straight on you'll probably keep going.

So, travelling sideways is not good: if you're able to turn at the last minute, try to hit things head-on.

If you need towing out you may regret not bringing a tow rope. If possible try to leave your car where it won't be a problem to other traffic and snowploughs.

Winter off-road driving

Pulling away

Ensure four-wheel drive is engaged, engage appropriate Terrain Response setting (if fitted) and use low-range gears (if fitted) when greater control is needed – this includes low-speed manoeuvres or tricky undulating terrain. Pulling away in the highest practical gear will provide more natural traction due to the reduced torque being transmitted to the wheels. If you drive a manual vehicle and keep stalling when attempting to move off it means you've selected a gear that's too high. Ensure differential locks are engaged and electronic traction systems enabled to yield the best chances of pulling away successfully.

There are occasions, especially when recovering a stuck vehicle, when disabling traction control systems can be beneficial, but it's usually best to attempt recovery with the systems

LEFT Clear forward vision, planning ahead, correct speed and controlled steering are a must on snow-covered tracks.

LEFT Wheelspin on climbs can cause the snow to become compacted, acting like ice.

enabled first, only switching them off if you've been unsuccessful. The traction systems that can occasionally be a hindrance are the variety that have the ability to reduce engine power as a result of traction loss – occasionally you'll need the ability to spin the wheels unhindered to provide maximum chances of recovery.

Making progress

OK, so you've managed to pull away successfully and now you need to maintain progress. Deep snow can hide hidden obstacles such as rocks, branches and frozen pools of water, so drive at a sensible pace, but keep momentum up where possible; plan as far ahead as you can to plot a route and prepare for unexpected hazards. If you're driving on a well-established track try to stick to the centre if possible to avoid hidden drainage ditches, etc.

Driving in rutted snow

If ruts have formed due to the action of previous vehicles, keep track of where your front wheels are pointing, as steering feel can be dramatically reduced. It's very common for drivers to apply a certain amount of steering lock without noticing and the car will happily continue to follow the path of the ruts – this isn't necessarily a problem unless the wheels do eventually find traction, as this could cause the vehicle to jump suddenly out of the ruts and off the track.

Climbing hills

If you absolutely need to climb a hill to reach your destination, remember to use the highest gear possible to give you the best chances of success and increase momentum. If you're struggling to make progress you can try 'steering for traction', which involves rapidly turning the steering about a quarter of a turn left and right repeatedly – you'll be surprised how effective this can be in really slippery conditions.

Controlling slides

Slides usually occur for one of two reasons: driver input or terrain. Keep all driver input as

BELOW The use of speed to overcome lack of traction can cause problems when increased traction suddenly becomes available.

ABOVE Descending steep downhill sections by driving in ruts will aid stability.

smooth and progressive as possible to make the most of available traction. If you do find yourself sliding while on the flat you'll probably be experiencing either understeer or oversteer.

Sliding downhill

If you're driving on a slope and start to slide downhill you'll need to react quickly to recover the situation. Avoid driving across a slope where possible: as a rule of thumb you should tackle these obstacles either straight up or straight down to gain maximum control. Remember that engine braking should be used to slow down the vehicle in preference to over-braking if no Terrain Response is fitted. However, in icy conditions even engine braking can cause a slide...

Sliding while slowing down

Always leave a serious amount of room to slow down, even with ABS fitted, which will usually lengthen your stopping distance to maintain steering control. Use this to your advantage to avoid hitting obstacles. Brake gently and progressively to reduce the chances of wheel lock, and remember that ABS is a reactive system, so it's best to avoid activating it at all if you can avoid it (because it means you've already caused at least one wheel to lock). If no ABS is fitted, consider alternative braking techniques such as cadence braking.

Clear snow from under the chassis

If your 4x4 is sitting on a bed of compacted snow it can be very difficult for the wheels to find grip, so clear any snow away from the underside of the car and around the wheels with a shovel. Cutting channels for the wheels to follow can also aid progress.

Reverse out the way you've come

This may seem tediously obvious, but it's often much easier to reverse out using the tracks that your own vehicle has created, rather than forging new ones by attempting to continue. This should usually be your first course of action.

Rocking backwards and forwards

If you're stuck in deep snow, sometimes a rhythmic rocking motion can be enough to free your vehicle. Alternate between a suitable forward gear and reverse, and attempt to start the car rocking forwards and backwards, thus creating a small area of flattened snow which can be used to create sufficient run-up to clear the obstacle.

Use traction aids

Sand ladders, snow chains, car mats and even cat litter can be helpful traction aids – use whatever you have at your disposal. Put it in front of the tyres in the desired direction of travel.

Towing

If you're well and truly in the deep stuff, towing is usually a much quicker and easier option than winching. Use tow ropes or straps that are suitably rated for the weight of the stranded vehicle and attach to approved recovery points. Drive the recovery car until the rope is tight, then stop. Then pull away gently while the driver of the stranded vehicle gently spins the wheels of the stuck car.

Water/wading

Adopt standard wading techniques, but beware of smashing into ice-covered water, as the broken bits of ice can build up at the front of your vehicle and damage the radiator.

ABOVE Driving into fresh snow can cause a build-up of snow underneath and in front of the vehicle, increasing rolling resistance.

Chapter Seventeen

How to tow on- and off-road

OPPOSITE It's a fact that 4x4s are the best tow vehicles. But towing successfully requires special skills.

ABOVE When buying a trailer, check the chassis number for legal reasons.

Four-wheel drives are the vehicles of choice for drivers who regularly tow trailers or caravans. It's no coincidence that the versatile Land Rover Discovery regularly picks up every towing award going, but many other 4x4s are excellent for the task too. Farmers, builders, caravan owners, horse owners, off-road triallers … anybody who needs to attach a heavy load to the tow hitch turns to the 4x4.

Their low-down torque, off-road ability and sheer physical bulk makes most 4x4s ideal if you want to tow a trailer, caravan or horse box. The low-down torque means that even heavy loads can be got moving easily, while the off-road

BELOW A correctly positioned tow-hitch above the tow ball.

ability means you're not going to get caught out by slippery grass and muddy gateways.

The physical bulk – in other words the overall gross vehicle weight – is vital when it comes to towing large loads. Larger 4x4s can legally tow a 3,500kg braked trailer. Put simply, the heavier the tow vehicle, the heavier the load you're allowed to tow – and most 4x4s are very heavy vehicles, with the larger ones tipping the scales at well over two tonnes. What's more, big 4x4s aren't skittish on the highway – which is important when you're towing.

Some 4x4s are supplied new with tow bar and associated electrics. Even those that don't come with a tow bar as standard have an optional tow pack, which many owners opt for. If you do decide to fit a tow bar yourself, make sure it's bolted to the correct points on the chassis and that the bolts are tightened to the manufacturer's recommended torque settings. Get an auto electrician to either install or check the electrics.

Having said all that, a heavily-laden trailer or caravan can pose problems when you attempt to drive it off-road, and special techniques are required. But we'll come to that shortly.

How to tow a trailer or caravan

To hitch a trailer to your 4x4, set the jockey wheel so that the coupling head of the trailer is about an inch higher than the tow ball. Many modern 4x4s have reversing cameras – some modern Land Rovers are fitted with new technology known as Tow Ball Assist, where cameras guide you to the correct position. Failing that, it's useful to have an assistant to carry out guidance duties.

With the trailer handbrake on, reverse until the coupling head is immediately above the tow ball, then slowly lower the jockey wheel until the locking mechanism engages. You should hear an audible click when it does, but it's important that you check it's engaged properly – jack up the jockey wheel to check if you're not sure.

The safety cable – also known as the breakaway cable – will activate the trailer's brakes in the event of the tow hitch failing. It's important that this is securely fixed to the correct point on your vehicle.

The electrics socket is vulnerable to off-

FAR LEFT Lift the handle to release the securing pin.

LEFT Make sure the breakaway cable is secured correctly.

LEFT Ensure that the electrical connections are clean and dry.

BELOW Check the vehicle and trailer VIN plates to make sure that axle loads and towing weights are within limits.

road abuse. Spray it with an electrical contact spray (or WD40, if pushed), and protect it when wading or driving deep mud by covering it with a strong plastic bag, secured with duct tape.

The maximum authorised mass – commonly known as the maximum kerbside weight – is clearly stated on the trailer's VIN plate. Never exceed these figures – to do so is both dangerous and illegal.

But before you go towing, check that *you're* legal. If you passed your driving test before 1 January 1997 you can drive a vehicle and trailer with a combined weight of up to 8.25 tons. If not, you'll have to take a special test.

Also remember the maximum speed limits for towing: 60mph on dual carriageways and motorways, 50mph on other roads.

Trailer and caravan theft is rife. To deter would-be thieves it's worthwhile having its identification number laser-cut into the chassis. VIN plates can be swapped, but it would be hard to get rid of this!

Towing off-road

The 4x4's reputation for towing is well deserved, but not even a good 4x4 can prevent you getting stuck if you attempt to tow a heavy trailer or caravan across soft ground. It's something that traps the unwary all the time. Dad towing the horse box for his daughter's gymkhana drives on to what looks like an innocuous grass field only for the wheels of the horse box to sink to their axles in a soft bit of

ABOVE Standard
50mm tow balls and
hitches have a limited
amount of lateral and
horizontal movement
in off-road conditions.

ground. Embarrassing, but only too common.

It catches out the experienced enthusiasts too. A few years back at a well-known 4x4 show a downpour turned the grassy fields into a quagmire. We can well remember some owners having to winch their heavily-laden 4x4s and caravans off the soggy site at the end of the weekend.

So you can see that towing a heavy trailer or caravan off-road does have its pitfalls. The biggest problem is that the laden trailer often weighs more than the 4x4 itself, yet it has poorer ground clearance (due to the need to keep the centre of gravity as low as possible) and narrow tyres on the axles, which will dig in deeper than the chunkier tyres on your 4x4. This means that places where you'd be able to drive without a problem in your 4x4 will see you stuck when you attempt to pull a heavy trailer through. The resistance of a trailer sinking into soft ground, where it's grounded chassis can act like an anchor, will be enough to see your 4x4 grind to a halt too.

And your problems don't end there. The

standard tow ball is not designed for extreme angles between the vehicle and trailer, neither laterally nor horizontally. This means that a heavily potholed track can cause real problems, as can abrupt undulations in the surface you're driving over. In the worst-case scenario, the forces generated can even break your tow bar or damage the trailer neck.

If you do a lot of towing off-road, or you decide to take your vehicle and trailer into extreme off-road situations – perhaps on an overland expedition across remote parts of Africa, where tarmac-covered roads are the exception – you may wish to fit a NATO-style tow hitch, developed by the military, which allows articulation both up and down and from side to side across all types of terrain without risk of failure. But if you don't want to swap tow hitches, the answer is to be very careful how you drive on uneven surfaces and on slopes.

The uneven surfaces you're likely drive off-road will also have an impact upon what you're carrying. Everything should be lashed down or secured – and in the case of a vehicle on a trailer, by means of very strong straps to prevent it from moving around. In a caravan, obviously, everything breakable should be stowed away carefully.

Happily, despite these apparent pitfalls, it's possible to tow heavy trailers off-road without coming to grief. As usual, it takes a bit of preparation and some thought on the part of the driver.

As in all off-road situations, always carry a recovery kit that includes a strong tow rope, shackles and shovel; and if you know it's going to be wet, some sort of tracking like sand mats will help. Ensure that the rope and shackles are rated high enough to pull eight tons – which is what you'll need if a bogged-down Defender 110 and laden trailer need to be extracted. Make sure the recovery points on your 4x4, and the vehicle recovering it, are also up to the job. If the combined weight is too much then think about unhitching the trailer and pulling vehicle and trailer out independently. Vince, who has decades of experience of towing big loads off-road in extreme circumstances, has even pulled his trailer gently forward under winch power when it's started to sink in wet ground and he didn't want to risk reversing his 4x4 on to the same patch.

Many caravans are fitted with what are known as 'movers', which drive the caravan wheels; you could lighten the caravan and, with a few friends pushing, use them to move the caravan to a more suitable place to hitch up.

One solution to driving soft ground in a 4x4 is to lower your tyre pressures to create a bigger 'footprint' and increase the area of rubber in contact with the ground. But under no circumstances should you lower the tyre pressures on your trailer wheels. They're of a different design and can easily be twisted off their rims under load if you attempt this. And always remember to blow your tyres back up to the recommended pressure before driving your rig on the road.

If in doubt, get out of your vehicle and assess the situation on foot. This particularly applies around field gateways, which get a lot of traffic and may be muddier than the rest of the field. You may have to take a good run-up in order to get the initial movement and momentum required to maintain traction through that treacherous gateway.

If possible, choose a route where the ground is firm and even. Of course, if it's a gateway there's probably no alternative but to drive through it, but before you do so think about reducing the weight of the load on the trailer. This may sound obvious, but if there are two horses in the horsebox, why not get them out and walk them through the difficult patch?

If possible get another driver to help. Two vehicles should give you enough power to get out of trouble, but again make sure your recovery points and equipment are up to it. You pull each other's trailers or caravans, one at a time.

In all off-road situations, select low gearbox and diff lock where fitted, plus any other traction-enhancing electronic devices your individual 4x4 may have. On modern Land Rovers (but not current Defenders), choose the appropriate setting on the Terrain Response dial (and the comparative setting on the systems fitted to other manufacturers' vehicles). Aim to drive in second or third gear and don't attempt to change gear on the move. The mere act of dipping the clutch will probably be enough to see you grind to a halt … and then you'll have real problems getting moving again. But slipping the clutch gently to feed in the power initially is acceptable.

At all times try to keep your tow vehicle and trailer in as straight a line as possible. Attempting tight turns will increase resistance and will probably get you stuck.

If you do get stuck, don't spin the wheels. Stop, gently reverse and try again at a less tight angle.

Weather plays a big part in the difficulties you're likely to encounter. Heavy rain can turn an otherwise innocuous grass field into a slippery ice rink once it gets wet. And don't forget that British weather can – and does – change! It's very easy to park up in glorious sunshine on a dry field and return in the afternoon to encounter a soggy quagmire. So always park on good, level ground and keep an eye on the weather.

There's no magic solution that'll stop you getting stuck when you tow your trailer or caravan off-road, but a little preparation and thought should prevent you getting into a situation where it could happen.

Chapter Eighteen

Where to go off-roading

OPPOSITE All types and all models of 4x4 (and their drivers) can have great fun tackling the natural challenges of a pay-and-play off-road site.

Your 4x4 is your passport to off-road adventure. Here are some of the best places to go…

Greenlaning

Over a century ago, a great revolution swept across the countryside. It was the internal combustion engine, and its arrival meant that the roads network of Europe, including the United Kingdom, had to change. Muddy, rutted lanes were OK for horses and carts, but they were no good for the new cars and lorries, which needed a firm, level surface to drive on.

Luckily for early motorists, another new invention – tarmac – solved the problem. In a very short time span, most of the country's lanes were covered in the stuff. But not all. Those that weren't are what we in the UK call green lanes.

Today, green lanes are one of the greatest pleasures of the countryside. Some are historic routes that date back thousands of years, others are old drovers' roads. All provide access to some of the best parts of the countryside – for everyone, and not just 4x4 drivers.

It wasn't until relatively recently – with the advent of the capable four-wheel drive in fact – that it was possible to drive most green lanes. Today, with more 4x4s on the road than ever before, some of these formerly quiet lanes have come under pressure. And that hasn't been helped by a minority of irresponsible 4x4 drivers treating them as playgrounds.

Green lanes fall into two categories – byways (Byways Open to All Traffic) and UCRs (Unclassified Country Roads). Both are public highways, where the rules of the road apply. Your vehicle must be taxed, insured and MoT'd

FAR LEFT Byways are open to all vehicles.

LEFT Byway signs come in all shapes and sizes, depending on the taste of the local county council's Highways department. The one on the far-left is from Northamptonshire, the one near-left Norfolk.

... and you certainly should *not* be deliberately getting stuck to test your winch or recovery techniques, no more than you would on a normal road.

To find out which ones you can legally drive, start by getting the relevant Ordnance Survey maps for your area. Then double-check with the local county council's Highways Department, who should be able to give you access to the definitive map for the county, with all rights of way marked. Your local library may also have a copy.

Be aware, though, that some local authorities place TROs (Traffic Restriction Orders) on some lanes in autumn and winter. These are usually lanes that traverse soft or muddy ground that can become badly rutted.

Understandably, many 4x4 owners are still worried about venturing on to green lanes, in case they get it wrong. We recommend joining a local Land Rover or 4x4 club, which do the groundwork for you by researching the legality of the lanes and even organise greenlaning trips. There are also professional companies that offer greenlaning tours to some of the best lanes in the most scenic areas. For example, Vince organises regular convoys to the green lanes of Wales.

LEFT Ordnance Survey maps offer good information on the location of greenlanes, but check with local authorities and off-road groups for up-to-date information.

You may also know a more experienced 4x4 driver who knows the local lanes and would be happy for you to join him on a greenlaning trip. It's best to travel in two vehicles, just in case one breaks down or gets stuck in the middle of nowhere. As always, bring along recovery gear, including a rated towrope, tree strop and shackles.

Although you're driving on a public road, you should still be using your off-road instincts – and by this we mean look, risk-assess and drive … in that order. Don't just aimlessly drive into ruts, water or mud if you don't know what lies ahead. If in any doubt, get out of the vehicle and walk the section before you drive it. Look for areas where the centre of the tracks have been scraped by the undersides of other vehicles. This is an indication that the ruts are too deep.

BELOW Many greenlanes are suitable for all types of 4x4 vehicles.

It's possible that you'll meet an irate farmer or rambler, who may tell you in no uncertain terms that you shouldn't be driving the lane. If so, be polite, show them your map and ask them why you shouldn't be there. If you encounter riders on horseback, pull over, switch off your engine and let them pass before you proceed.

Whatever you do, don't drive as though you're in the Dakar Rally or a hill rally stage. As far as speed goes, Vince's old adage to drive as slow as possible and as fast as necessary applies. You may need a little extra momentum to get you across an area of soft ground, but always be aware of other users.

Abide by the country code at all times, which means closing gates and taking your litter home.

Luckily, groups like GLASS (the Green Lane Association) and LARA (the Land Access and Recreation Association) already do a great job in putting across our case and fighting against green lane closures. That's why you need the very latest OS mapping.

Remember that byways are public roads and all rules of the road apply, so make sure you and your vehicle are fully road-legal.

Off-road sites

Byways aren't the sort of places where four-wheel-drive owners should come out and test their toys. If you want to try mud-plugging, rock crawling, hill climbs and winching you should head for one of the many pay-and-play off-road sites dotted all over the country.

Here there are no rules of the road to worry about except the safety ones, but that doesn't mean you should drive around like a nutcase putting your vehicle and your safety at risk. As you read this book you'll see that off-road driving entails certain skills that you'll need in order to get the most out of it.

But certainly the pay-and-play site is the place to learn and polish those skills. As the name suggests, you pay a modest entrance fee and come to test the capabilities of both yourself and your vehicle.

Different sites on different types of terrain mean that you have a great choice of challenges, according to the venue. One might be mainly sandy; another heavy, sticky clay; another full of boulders. All are great fun!

ABOVE Off-roading at a Land Rover Experience Centre or similar venue is a wonderful way to learn the skills and techniques required.

BELOW 4x4 'fun days' take place all over the country at off-road sites that are open to the public, enabling you to use your own vehicle off-road.

Off-road competitions

These are organised at local and national level by Land Rover and 4x4 clubs and range from trials aimed at beginners staged by local Land Rover clubs through to fast and furious off-road motorsport in specially-prepped racing machines.

Check out the events pages of 4x4 magazines for what's on in your area and consider joining your local club, where you'll meet like-minded people and gain access to off-road events. Some also organise green lane outings.

Club trialling

A 4x4 trial usually consists of eight or more sections, each of which requires a driver to follow a course over arduous and awkward terrain, defined by up to ten pairs of marker canes. The canes are numbered 10 (Start),

9, 8, etc down to 1 (Finish), though 'blank' canes may be included to further define the route. You're scored by how far you get before any part of your vehicle touches one of the canes. These events are invaluable in gaining experience on how to drive off-road in all types of conditions and on all types of terrain – they're where I started! There are several classes, from RTVs (Road Taxed Vehicles) to road-going vehicles and under-age drivers.

Comp Safari racing

Comp Safari is all about speed, with various classes for different vehicles from nearly standard with safety modifications to all cross-country buggies built specially for such events. You compete against each driver/vehicle in your class, racing against the clock around a course designed to slow you down.

Those who have competed in a Comp Safari

ABOVE Off-road racing is fantastic fun, and a good spectator sport, though venues are few and far between, and specialist vehicles are required.

BELOW Long-distance and 'rally-raid' events are held all over Europe, but mainly at desert locations.

off-road race are well aware of the thrill you get when you drive a vehicle that's correctly prepared for the purpose of speed across country. In Official MSA races all entries are checked by an official MSA scrutineer prior to every race. You're then permitted to drive the vehicle to its maximum within the course limitations, which isn't always as easy as it seems.

Winching challenges

These events involve using the pulling power of one or more winches to get your vehicle to places no sane driver would consider attempting, like through deep swamps or to the top of sheer cliffs. The art of winching successfully – and, most importantly, safely – is a whole new set of skills that you must learn in order to succeed at this game.

Many challenges involve driving through deep water, so diesel engines reign supreme, assisted of course by a properly fitted snorkel with 100% watertight seals. Meanwhile,

gearbox and axle breathers need extended pipes to roof level to keep water out.

Challenging times ahead...

It was probably the Camel Trophy that started it all. Through the 1980s and '90s, teams from all over the world competed in what was the greatest 4x4 event ever held – involving Land Rovers and sheer human endurance in some of the most inhospitable corners of our planet.

The early Camel Trophy events were unashamed mud-plugging extravaganzas, often through virgin rainforest in exotic places like Sumatra, Papua New Guinea, Zaire, Brazil, Borneo and Madagascar. Back in the 1980s such behaviour hardly raised an eyebrow, but environmental concerns and political correctness through the 1990s saw the organisers under pressure to dilute the mud-plugging aspects and include other activities like kayaking and mountain climbing.

BELOW You don't necessarily have to be a driver on an event – co-drivers are always required.

But the spirit of the Camel Trophy lives on in extreme challenge events, which are still held all over the world. The Portuguese in particular love tough off-road challenges. The heavily forested and rugged centre of their country is the perfect setting for this type of event, and attracts drivers of extreme 4x4s from all over Europe. Russia, too, has in recent years become an exciting destination for extreme challenge fans.

In the UK you won't get the chance to winch your way through a dense jungle or up a Portuguese mountainside, but you can be assured that the extreme challenges held on these shores are every bit as tough and technical as those found anywhere else in the world. In fact it's here that you're likely to see the finest exponents of the art of winching, as the most challenging features will have been specially created by the event organisers at a specialist off-road site.

Most of the UK's tough challenges are staged in the autumn and winter – presumably so that the mud is deeper and stickier! Many of these events are advertised in the 4x4 press and you can also check out Simon Buck's Devon 4x4 website (www.devon4x4.com), which has a special section devoted to forthcoming 4x4 events.

Europe

Of course, many 4x4 owners like to take their vehicles abroad to explore off-road possibilities in foreign climes. Most European countries are blessed with plenty of off-road sites, very similar to the pay-and-play sites in the UK, and the advantage of going to Europe is that you get to drive the sort of terrain you wouldn't find on home soil – great, craggy mountains under a clear blue sky, for starters!

Unfortunately, the laws on greenlaning are as confused in Europe as they are in the UK. In France, access to rural tracks depends on the region you're in. In some you're free to drive virtually anywhere, while in others you may

BELOW Specialist companies organise 'tag along' off-road adventures in the UK, Europe and North Africa. This photo shows Paklenica Gorge in Croatia during a trip organised by Protrax.

need the written permission of the local mayor! To be on the safe side, always make enquiries locally before putting a tyre on any track you're unsure about.

In Holland and Germany greenlaning is illegal, but in Spain and Portugal there's a wealth of tracks that anyone can drive. Austria used to be a great destination for greenlaners, with fantastic mountain tracks, but in recent years new anti-4x4 legislation has closed most of them off. It's the same situation in Slovenia, but in nearby Croatia there are still lanes you're entitled to drive, although it's best to seek the services of a local guide, as many traverse areas still blighted by landmines left over from the Balkans conflict of the 1990s.

In Italy the roads through most of the mountainous regions are often little more than tracks, which provide great legal driving for 4x4 owners. The tracks of the Alps in northern Italy, close to the French border, are particularly stunning when it comes to views.

In Greece there are companies that offer amazing off-road excursions coupled with visits to historical and cultural sites before camping for the night on a secluded beach next to the sea.

Scandinavia has some good tracks, but laws vary from country to country. There's very little greenlaning in Denmark, for example, but plenty of off-road sites. In Sweden the forest tracks can be driven with a special permit, and the annual Sweden Off-Road Tour is embarked on by 4x4 drivers from all over Europe who converge on the country for a trip to the Arctic Circle driving off-road as much as possible. But the most exciting Scandinavian country for Land Rover fans has to be Iceland.

Today, the most exciting destinations for greenlaning adventures are probably the former Eastern Bloc countries like Poland, Hungary, Romania, the Czech Republic and Bulgaria, where mountains, vast forests and a seemingly relaxed attitude to driving down country tracks means fun for 4x4 drivers. But remember that criminal gangs still roam some Eastern European countries, so travel in small convoys to be safe. And always check on local laws before venturing off-road.

Worldwide

Beyond Europe, there are plenty of destinations where 'greenlaning' isn't a hobby, it's a way of life … because in some poorer countries most roads aren't surfaced with tarmac, so in effect they're all rough tracks, very similar to the byways you find in most parts of Wales (except it doesn't rain so much).

Africa is the nearest neighbouring continent to the UK – and certainly the easiest to get to. To take your 4x4 overland to Morocco, you can drive through France and Spain and get on the ferry across the Straits of Gibraltar. To get to Tunisia, you drive to Marseilles (France) or Genoa (Italy) and do the same.

For many years Vince has been leading guided tours to Morocco and he still reckons it's the most dramatic and diverse country in the world. You get to drive through cedar forests, the High Atlas Mountains and the Sahara Desert in a matter of days, with exciting new vistas opening in front of your vehicle at seemingly every turn! Access is good, but be sure you respect local culture and traditions in the places you drive through.

Tunisia is sandier than Morocco but perhaps not as dramatic. But there's plenty to interest the adventurous 4x4 owner, including the movie sets where *Star Wars* was filmed!

For the more adventurous traveller, you can press on beyond northern Africa to explore the rest of this fascinating continent, but it's most definitely not a case of jumping in your 4x4 and driving south. There are war zones to avoid and countries where Westerners are at best not welcome, at worst in serious danger. Always plan and research any such overland trip very carefully and check with the Foreign Office for the latest information on the countries you may be driving through.

In reality, very few 4x4 owners embark on such long overland trips, which take many months to complete and months or even years of specialist preparation for themselves and their vehicles. Most opt instead for fly-drives to places like Namibia, Botswana and South Africa, where you get off the plane and into a fully-equipped 4x4 – usually a Land Rover or Toyota – which will be your home for the next week or two as you explore the fascinating

countryside, and sleep securely in your roof tent at night with lions and elephants as your nearest neighbours!

In Asia there are again plenty of places where unsurfaced roads give the 4x4 driver plenty of scope for exploring. South-East Asia in particular is a destination where you can combine driving in tropical rainforests with a sophisticated beach holiday. The same applies to Australia, where once you're out of the cities and in the Outback you're guaranteed a unique experience. The deserts in the centre of this vast country are some of the loneliest places on the planet. Dave has driven across the Simpson Desert – so remote that he couldn't pick up a single station on the car radio – and reckons it was probably the most amazing off-road adventure in his life.

The ideal way of getting to drive off-road in far off countries is to drive your own 4x4 there,

of course. And while an overland trek to South-East Asia is possible, it'll probably take you a year to get there, and obviously few people can afford to do that. The answer is to have your vehicle shipped to your destination, and you join it by flying there.

Be aware, though, that it's a complicated affair in most countries. In some you literally have to 'import' and 'export' your own vehicle every time you cross the borders… and the smaller the country, the more bureaucratic this process seems to become! Be prepared for a lot of red tape – and, of course, to be without your beloved Land Rover for a long time. It can take six weeks to get it shipped to Australia.

There are shipping companies that'll do it for you, though. You then have the choice of sending it as deck cargo or in a container. The latter is more expensive, but it's probably the kindest option for your vehicle.

ABOVE For the more adventurous, safari holidays into the Moroccan Sahara are not as expensive as you may think.

Navigation

– don't go anywhere until you've read this!

Outside on your drive is your 4x4. Today you used it to drop the kids off at school. Last weekend you went greenlaning. A couple of weeks ago you took it round an off-road site. But you know that, given half a chance, you could drive it round the world.

That, after all, is the essence of owning a 4x4 in the first place. It can take you to the places other vehicles would baulk at.

But what would you do when you got there? How would you find your way around in a Third World country where good maps are a luxury that hasn't yet arrived? There are a lot of wilderness places in this world where the cost of getting lost is your life. You see? – driving round the globe isn't as easy as you thought.

'What about GPS?' we can hear you say. Well, I heard you loud and clear. But although finding your exact location on the planet is straightforward with satellite navigation, it can let you down. What happens if the batteries go flat, or the electronic wizardry dies? Then you're literally lost.

Maps and compasses have been around a long time, and until fairly recently they were the

BELOW Whether travelling in the UK, Europe, or anywhere else worldwide, detailed planning of your trip is a must.

only serious way to navigate. But to those of us who sat at the back of the class and didn't pay attention during geography lessons, they remain a bit of a black art. That's why GPS is seen by many as the new black – the fashion accessory for your Land Rover that also serves a useful purpose. Just let technology do the hard work, eh?

We love maps. They're more than just sheets of paper with information on – every one has a multitude of stories to tell. Better than any bestseller, we'd say. Perhaps that's why studying them is called map-reading.

In the UK we're lucky. We've got Ordnance Survey maps, which are the best in the world. They're accurate, inexpensive and readily available. Once you're abroad, Michelin maps are an excellent first choice for driving on tarmac and off-road in former French colonies like Morocco. Like OS maps in the UK, they can be purchased at reasonable cost virtually everywhere.

Pick up the OS Landranger map for your area. It's 1:50,000 scale, which means that 1.25in on the map represents one mile on the ground. Just look at your neighbourhood: the road you live in will be there. Look closely and you'll see the local churches, pubs and even phone boxes. See those green bits? They're wooded areas. Look at them closely and you'll even by able to see whether the trees are deciduous, coniferous or a mixture of both. Even orchards and greenhouses are marked. They're that detailed!

Now look at the brown contour lines. They show the level of the land. Where the contour lines are close together it means there's a steep hill. Where they're a long way apart, it means the land is fairly level. In the flat fens of Lincolnshire, Cambridgeshire and West Norfolk you'll struggle to find any contour lines at all. The blue lines show the courses of streams and rivers, thick black lines show railway lines (thinner ones show power lines).

There's not room here to list all the features you can find on an OS map. See for yourself in the 'Legends' area (that's the key information on the right-hand side of your map).

But to drivers – particularly 4x4 owners – the most important information is the roads and rights of way. OS maps list them all, from motorways (blue) through main roads (red), minor roads (yellow) and tracks. They even show the green lanes you can probably drive – but don't rely 100% on the information you see. The status of these lanes change. As we've already recommended earlier, before you go greenlaning it's important that you get the most up-to-date information from your local Land Rover club's rights of way officer, or the Highways Department of the county council.

There's no excuse for ever getting lost in the UK. Armed with a map, a compass and the knowledge of how to read an OS map you'll soon be on course again.

But that's not always the case in foreign countries. Many poorer countries are covered by maps that are inaccurate or decades out of date. Since many of them were drawn up by the military back in colonial times, that's hardly surprising. In North Africa I've driven along what should have been an empty road only to arrive at a large, modern town that didn't exist 50 years ago when the map I was using was drawn up by French cartographers!

There are even parts of the world where no maps of any value are available at all. And there are some areas, like the Sahara Desert for example, where there are so few features – not even any roads – that maps are of little help (although a compass is, of course). Many UK travellers are surprised when they go abroad and discover that foreign countries don't use the UK's OS mapping system...

Experienced travellers know that it's essential to purchase the appropriate maps long before their journey – if only to plan it out beforehand. For many years, Stanfords in London has been the Mecca for people purchasing specialist maps for every destination around the globe. These days, of course, that facility is available online. Log on to www.stanfords.co.uk and explore!

It's on occasions like this that we turn to GPS. In case you're one of the few people who still don't know, that stands for Global Positioning System, and it does just what it says – it tells you exactly where you are by reading signals bounced back from satellites in space.

A wide range of navigational instruments and software is available to help you navigate off-road almost anywhere around the world.

There are 24 GPS satellites up there, orbiting the earth at 33,000km. The important thing is that your GPS unit back on terra firma seeks out those satellites. It needs to lock on to four of them to get a really accurate fix on your position (three will usually suffice, but four is better).

On his trips to Morocco, Vince uses his Garmin 196 GPS to trace his route across the desert where there are no tracks. Then he stores the route in the unit's memory for future use. It's really handy if you want to return to a particularly interesting area – or avoid an area of soft sand or difficult, rocky terrain. However, these days companies like Garmin, Fugawi and others offer specialist, detailed maps of most countries in the world.

Ordnance Survey maps show both their own grid references (Eastings and Northings) plus latitude/longitude, which is used worldwide.

If you've never taken a grid reference, here's how to do it. Open an OS map and you'll see it's divided up into little squares by thin blue vertical and horizontal lines. Each of those lines has a number at the end of it. The numbers along the top and bottom of the map are Eastings, the ones down the sides are Northings.

Having found the place on the map you want to give a grid reference for, locate the first vertical line (Easting) to the left of it. Say it's 19. Now estimate by eye how many tenths of the square your spot is away from the line. If it's halfway, that's 5.

Now locate the first horizontal line from below the point and note the Northing number. Say it's 11. Again estimate how many tenths away. Let's say this time that it's 3.

That means your grid reference is 195 113.

It probably sounds more complicated than it is. Practise and you'll soon get the hang of it.

In the UK you don't normally need a compass. In daylight in most places you'll get by nicely with your OS map. But if you're in the wilds – say, out on a mountain – in a blizzard, fog or just total darkness, you could soon become disorientated. A compass will tell you where north, south, east, west and all the bits between are. So at least you'll be able to get a direction fix and find your way to safety.

But a word of warning. Compasses work by pointing to the magnetic North Pole (which is actually a shade to the north-west of the grid 'north' used on most maps, including OS sheets). That means to get an accurate compass reading you should get out of your vehicle and stand several feet away. Yes, even if it's raining and blowing a gale! That's because the average 4x4 has lots of bits of metal, electrics and various magnetic fields that could affect the reading.

If you're going round the world a GPS is a wise investment, but always bring along a compass, just in case you drop it or it simply goes dead on you. As I said earlier, a featureless desert is no place to get lost. But if you do, a compass will enable you to head off in the right direction without going around in circles.

Finally, remember that GPS isn't infallible. In the middle of the jungle, or even a dense pine forest in East Anglia, you'll find it hard if not impossible to pick up signals from enough satellites to give you an accurate location fix. We've also been in mountainous areas and quarries where minerals, metals or whatever in the strata have made GPS go haywire.

Give us a map and compass any day … but we'll also take along a GPS with the relevant country information.

Is this the future?

These days, companies like Memory-Map combine the latest computer technology with GPS and digital mapping, so that the terrain featured on your OS mapping software unfolds on your GPS monitor as you drive along.

Long ago, when early but inquisitive humans first began to explore their world, they used the stars to navigate. They had to, really – it was that or get lost. Celestial navigation, as it came to be known, ruled supreme for thousands of years. But it had one drawback – you could only navigate by the stars on clear nights. Perhaps that's why Spain and Portugal produced some of the world's best explorers; in cloudy Britain you didn't stand a chance.

Today, the nomadic tribes of the Sahara still navigate by the stars. But for most of the rest us the world has moved on at breakneck

pace. Maps and compass have already been rivalled if not replaced by ever-evolving GPS systems. And now there's even a system which marries the best of GPS and maps with the latest computer technology.

Memory-Map is software that, once installed in your computer, allows you not only to access the best maps in the world on your screen, but also allows you to do things with them you'd only have dreamed of in the past.

At the click of a mouse, you can convert a standard OS map into a 3D topographical chart, with the software converting those contour lines into 'real' hills, mountains and valleys. Then you can plot your route, save it and store it for future reference. You can even attach notes and pictures taken on your journey.

Using GPS, you can see exactly where you are on the map – and what obstacles lie ahead. Just imagine how useful that would be on your next greenlaning trip!

Besides being able to load digital versions of standard Ordnance Survey Landranger (1:50,000) and Explorer (1:25,000) maps, you can also use A-Z city street plans, marine and aviation charts, plus the many thousands of other maps available throughout the world in digital format.

Memory-Map can be used on a standard PC laptop or pocket PC. The latter is particularly good on the move, as it can be mounted on the dashboard for easy viewing by driver or passenger/navigator.

Mobile phone network coverage around the world is very good (provided you've set your phone for 'roaming', of course…). But there are locations in the middle of nowhere where you won't be able to get a signal, so if you're travelling overland you may want to consider investing in a satellite phone. Once very expensive, the cost of these items has fallen dramatically in recent years, and for your own safety and peace of mind they're well worth having.

CB radio sets are good for communication between vehicles, and also help relieve boredom on long journeys, but be aware that in some countries like Morocco and Tunisia they're illegal.

Chapter Nineteen

Professional training

OPPOSITE Professional off-road training being undertaken by clients at one of six Land Rover Experience centres around the UK, this one being the East of England Land Rover Experience at Rockingham Castle.

ABOVE It is important to learn about forward observation, as well as steering, throttle and clutch control.

BELOW Gearchanging techniques are also fundamentally important – how, when and why.

You may wonder why we're writing a chapter on professional training when this book is supposed to be teaching you all the skills you need to drive your 4x4 off-road. Well, we don't see the two as mutually exclusive: certainly the theoretical information you require is complete, but putting it in practice to become a competent off-road driver will take time. You can't beat experience, but you'll get more skilled quicker if you seek professional training. If you're somebody who depends upon off-road driving for your job, professional training is probably compulsory.

It's equally useful for enthusiasts. Professional tuition will help turn you into a driver capable of tackling the toughest challenges. A day spent at a professional 4x4

training centre will help you understand your 4x4 transmission system, different off-road situations and, of course, to address your own limitations and fears. All this will help you to get the very best out of your vehicle.

Vince has been an off-road driving instructor for more than two decades. He even helped teach co-author Dave to drive off-road, many years ago. He says: 'I'm obviously biased – I've been a professional off-road instructor for many years – but I can assure you that proper training in off-road driving techniques will enhance your enjoyment as well as ensure the safety of yourself, your passengers and your vehicle.

It doesn't matter whether you're driving a local off-road site or across a continent – proper training will help you make the most out of your own skills and your vehicle. An experienced instructor will be able to help you achieve just that.

Let's look at a typical pay-and-play day at an off-road site. You turn up in your 4x4 and get to drive up and down hills, side slopes, ruts, water and, of course, mud. But you're not sure about the very steepest hills and deepest water – are you and your vehicle capable of tackling the biggest challenges? So you either avoid them, or take a risk – and you should never do that. Think how much better you'd enjoy your driving day if you were confident in your capability. It's important to master the skills that'll put a smile on your face and prevent things going wrong – and professional training can do that.

As a driver you have a duty of care for your passengers, so you need to gain experience and learn about your vehicle and the techniques required to tackle a variety of terrain and off-road situations. Another benefit is that fewer breakages occur with a better understanding of how the vehicle works, which will in turn help your pocket!

For many people, driving off-road isn't a weekend hobby – it's an important part of their work. Farmers and forestry workers, utility companies, aid agencies ... they all rely upon using 4x4 vehicles to travel off-road for their everyday jobs, so comply with the Health & Safety Executive's requirement for 'adequate training' and the Provision for Use of Work

Equipment Regulations (PUWER), which require employees to be certificated following training by qualified off-road instructors.

A typical off-road driving course will be conducted by knowledgeable instructors, and will start with a classroom briefing on 4x4 basics and safety. It should then continue behind the wheel with the skills you've read about in this book, namely:

- 4x4 mechanicals.
- Use of diff-lock and traction enhancement devices.
- Ground-reading skills (look and risk-assess).
- Understanding torque and power relationships.
- Throttle and clutch control.
- Vehicle loading and security.
- Side slope capability.
- Hill climbs and descents.
- Failed hill climbs.
- Understanding momentum.
- Gear selection.
- Mud and ruts.
- Wading.
- Steering.
- Passenger safety.
- Tyre choice.
- Environmental issues.
- Final debriefing.

Vince says he'd also recommend courses that offer one-to-one tuition. Sharing a vehicle and instructor with other people will dilute the first-hand experience you should be getting, although two to one is acceptable.

There are also independent off-road centres that offer a similar service, although you have to be careful who you choose to teach you! Unfortunately, there's no law in this country to prevent any individual calling himself an off-road driving instructor. This is clearly potentially dangerous, as an inexperienced instructor could put you in a position where you and your vehicle are in danger. However, professional instructors should be accredited by BORDA (the British Off-Road Driving Association), LANTRA (the national training organisation for land-based industries – its name isn't an acronym, but is made up from the words 'Land' and 'Training'), or the Land

Rover Experience, which has centres across the UK.

There are also courses to cover more specialised aspects of off-road driving – notably winch and recovery training, trailer handling and navigation skills. Some offer niche training like dynamic driving and off-road racing.

As in all areas of life, training makes you better at what you do. Training, as a term, goes hand-in-hand with development, so don't be too proud to admit that you require the odd bit of training here and there. An afternoon spent with a professional will bypass hours of trial and error. Also, remember that vehicle technology changes rapidly, and professional training will help you understand how the new electronic traction management aids work.

ABOVE Under guidance, you will be able to familiarise yourself with most of the obstacles and terrain types that you are likely to encounter off-road in the UK and Europe.

BELOW You will also have the opportunity to learn about winching equipment and techniques safely, in a controlled environment.

Chapter Twenty

And finally ...

OPPOSITE Responsible 4x4 owners driving a byway on a summer's day when the firm track surface will not be damaged by their passing.

How to be a green off-roader

Forget that propaganda about 'gas-guzzling 4x4s' – you can be an environmentally friendly 4x4 owner if you follow this advice.

To begin with, simply by owning a Land Rover you're endorsing a company that does its utmost to protect the environment, with green schemes like its carbon offset plan, which compensates for the CO_2 the company's manufacturing processes generate. Other manufacturers, at home and abroad, have embarked on similar environmentally-friendly programmes.

BELOW Do not take detours and make your own tracks when greenlaning.

But being a green 4x4 owner means more than that, of course. Let's look at the ways you can be environmentally friendly when you go greenlaning or off-roading…

Vehicle maintenance

Being green starts before you leave home. Is your vehicle properly serviced and maintained? For example, are the fuel injectors in good condition? All of these things make a big difference to fuel economy, which in turn means lower emissions and you doing the environment a big favour.

Do your vehicle's gearbox, diffs or axles leak oil? If so, get them fixed. All seals should be in good condition. Never go wading through rivers or streams if there's a risk of leaving a noxious oil slick behind.

Incidentally, if you do your own servicing and maintenance, make sure you dispose of old engine oil, batteries, brake pads etc in an environmentally friendly way. Old oil, for example, must never be tipped down the drain because it can cause catastrophic pollution if it reaches a watercourse. It's also illegal and will result in you making an unscheduled court appearance if you're caught.

Always dispose of worn-out components correctly. If you're not sure how to do this, contact your local council for advice.

A haze of blue smoke in the wake of your Land Rover means it's burning oil, which is definitely bad for the planet. Clouds of black smoke means the mixture is wrong, so get it fixed.

By the way, if you're driving a thirsty petrol-engined 4x4, have you considered having an LPG conversion fitted? There isn't the big financial incentive in switching to gas that there used to be, thanks to the Government increasing duty on LPG, but it's definitely kinder to the environment. The downside is that the LPG must be stored in tanks that either take up boot space or fit under the vehicle, behind the sills, which makes them vulnerable to knocks. The latter are obviously a no-no for the off-roader.

Wheels and tyres

Those big, chunky, off-road tyres may look the part, but are they necessary? The drag factor alone can reduce your fuel consumption by 7–8mpg compared to standard wheels and road-biased tyres, as we've found out in the past. Vince once removed the mud tyres from his off-road diesel Land Rover Discovery and was amazed to see an improvement in fuel consumption from 18mpg to 27mpg.

Are your tyres inflated to the recommended pressures? Not only do under- or over-inflated tyres mar your fuel consumption figures, they also wear more quickly, which is definitely bad for the environment (as well as your pocket).

Driving techniques

Keep your revs low to minimise emissions. Never rev the engine unnecessarily and, if you're at a standstill waiting for your mate to climb the hill, switch off the engine even if it's only for a few minutes. It makes a difference.

If your Land Rover has a diff lock or modern traction enhancement devices like Terrain Response, use them thoughtfully on low-traction surfaces to avoid excessive wheelspin.

If the green lane you're planning to drive is very wet or muddy, turn back and don't tackle it. Causing deep ruts is definitely unfriendly to the environment.

When you're driving green lanes, keep to the proper route. Don't make detours and damage the ground, and never use green lanes as a

BELOW Always check that it is legal to drive along any route that you anticipate taking. Just because there are wheel tracks present, it doesn't mean that it is legal to drive there. *(Land Rover)*

ABOVE If you find no obvious tracks on a lane indicated on your map, it may be that the lane has been downgraded and is no longer legal to drive.

RIGHT At certain times of the year, some lanes in certain areas have temporary closures to protect them. Always respect these closures.

playground to test your new winch, etc. Not only does it damage the environment, it could get vehicles banned from the route – something that's happened all too often in the past, thanks to a minority of irresponsible 4x4 drivers.

Respect the Country Code, which means, amongst other things, closing gates after you've driven through them, and always taking all your litter home with you. Not only does other people's rubbish look unsightly, it can also be lethal to farm animals and wildlife.

The future

Being a responsible, environmentally aware 4x4 owner will help to improve the image of off-roaders. In the UK we've unjustly suffered a bad image, mainly through prejudice and mischief by activists who play on the misconception that 4x4s are owned by rich people who don't need four-wheel drive. While it's true that some urban 4WD owners – the so-called 'Chelsea Tractor' drivers – never get their tyres dirty, research

has proven that the majority of 4x4 owners do use that all-terrain ability. This isn't just hearsay: when the engine management systems of modern 4x4s are plugged into computers at the garage at service time, it's possible to determine how often the Terrain Response knob has been used in various settings, including 'Mud and Ruts', for example.

The truth is that 4x4s are more popular than ever, in all corners of the world. The versatility of these vehicles is recognised everywhere and recreational off-roading is becoming more popular than ever. Research carried out by *Land Rover Monthly* magazine reveals that around two-thirds of new 4x4 owners plan to take their new cars off-road or on long overland expeditions. This is borne out by Vince's experience running off-road courses and leading convoys of 4x4s across Europe to North Africa. He's been doing this for many years, but gets larger numbers of new customers every year.

Manufacturers of 4x4 vehicles know this, of course. That's why they're constantly

ABOVE Right-of-way greenlanes provide you and your family with access to some amazing scenery and locations, but don't abuse this right.

engaged in developing and launching new models. They're also developing exciting new technology that makes their 4x4s more capable, reliable and economical.

It's our opinion that 4x4 ownership will continue to grow and ever larger numbers of people will enjoy the experience of taking them off-road. If that's you, we hope you've enjoyed this book – and wish you plenty of enjoyable driving. Happy off-roading!

LEFT Off-roading does not always have to mean big 4x4s with big wheels and lights everywhere!

BELOW Modern Land Rover models, such as this Evoque, have fantastic looks coupled with incredible off-road capability.

Glossary

Bump-stops – Rubber pads designed to protect a vehicle from the violent bottoming out caused when the suspension runs out of upward travel without fully absorbing the energy of the stroke in the shock absorbers.

Cadence braking – Bringing a vehicle to a controlled stop by putting it into low gear and applying lots of short, sharp applications of the brake pedal in rapid sequence.

Corrugations – Nickname for the regular bumps found on dirt and desert roads.

Cross-axled – Situation where one front wheel is in a deep depression at the same time as the rear wheel on the opposite side.

Deadman anchor – A winching anchor constructed from a log or spare tyre buried in the ground with the winch line connected to it at its centre.

Engine braking – Reduction in engine speed caused by the combination of a low gear coupled with the engine's inability to get rid of exhaust gases because the engine isn't being revved high enough. It results in the engine reducing vehicle speed to a crawl.

Feathering the throttle – Term used to describe constant, gentle on-and-off use of the throttle, with small increases in engine revs to help keep a vehicle moving forward without breaking traction.

Hydraulic lock – Effect caused when one or more engine cylinders becomes filled with water, and the piston, trying to rise in the cylinder, makes contact with the water and can't move any further.

KERR – Kinetic energy recovery rope.

KERS – Kinetic energy recovery strap.

Limiting straps – Means of restricting the suspension's downward travel within safe limits for the linkages and shock absorbers to accommodate.

MT – Type of tyre designed for use in 'extreme mud'.

Ramp breakover – The angle between two imaginary lines, intersecting at the centre-point of the underneath of the body, taken from the back of the front wheel and the front of the back wheel (see diagram on P72). This angle determines the vehicle's ability to crest a hill without grounding out.

Snatch strap – Another name for a KERS.

Snorkel – Nickname for a raised air intake.

Steering for traction – Driving technique that involves rapidly turning the steering wheel about a quarter of a turn left and right repeatedly,

Wind-up – A phenomenon which can occur on part-time and permanent 4WD vehicles when 4WD or diff-lock is engaged. It is caused by the transfer box delivering equal percentages of torque to both front and rear axles when, in fact, when cornering, each axle required differing amounts of torque. This places excessive strain on the transmission components, and can cause breakages.

Witness marks – Marks on the ground indicating that the nether regions of a vehicle have scraped across the surface.